# Endorsement Career Prospectors (Job Assistance Ministry)

Most often hard-working professionals overlook the self-assurance needed to make connections, calls or to take action. Career Prospectors provides the resources for support groups and developing technical skills in order to increase the self-confidence needed to act. In the process they become comfortable being authentic and able to reveal not just their experiences but their true self to potential employers. Surviving Career Transition by Allen Pickett captures the challenges and progress of such job seekers.

*Charlie Wood, Founder Career Prospectors*

The job search process is very stressful, fraught with financial worries, self-doubt, and anxiety for the future, clearly an emotional roller coaster ride. So how to stay motivated and focused during these challenging times? Allen Pickett has created a scriptural guide to help us navigate the career transition process. It is an inspiring guide to first understand our God-given gifts and talents, and then develop a career objective and ultimately our vision for the future that are true to our values and beliefs. So, if you are searching for a new job or just want to re-examine your career and life trajectory, this book is a must read.

*Ed Landry, Founder Job Assistance Ministry*

# Surviving Career Transition

40 lessons on how men and women in the Bible respond to unemployment, waiting and disappointment

by
Allen L. Pickett

Patti Law, Editor

# Dedication

The inspiration for this book came from my involvement in Career Prospectors. This is a job seeking group in Richmond, VA for people dealing with job loss or looking to improve their work situation. It is completely volunteer-led and offers help to write a resume, use social media, develop networking skills, create accountability, and learn from industry-related round tables.

A year ago I was trying to figure out how I could contribute to this group using my unique skills as a pastor. I felt God led me to develop a resource to view unemployment, waiting, and disappointment through the lens of Scripture. So I began writing a weekly blog, and I invited my friends to come on Friday mornings to read a Scripture passage and my blog. We then discussed how the message impacted us and how we might apply the principles to our lives.

I have been encouraged through studying God's Word as I discern my own way, and I hope you will find yourself in the Bible passages and stories that I share.

I dedicate this book to my friends who are struggling to keep their wits about them, maintain a positive attitude, and find answers to questions that they were not even asking before they were given this gift of unemployment.

# Acknowledgements

I would like to express deep appreciation to my friend Patti Law who spent many hours in a very short amount of time editing my book. She was able to add grammatical and word choices that helped my thoughts make sense to the reader. Also, an old friend, Bobby Kelland took a final look finding important details throughout which will enhance your reading experience.

Many of my Career Prospector friends read and discussed with me the blogs which became the daily readings. Their input and advice was invaluable.

# Preface

Whenever we read the Bible, we study it through a particular lens. My current issues and dilemmas cause me to ask questions and seek answers that are beyond me and my experience. The Bible, although ancient in authorship, is written about people. And people don't change, not really. We come at everything with an agenda. I hear your compliments and criticisms through the lens of my emotional security. I read the newspaper looking for views that support my own. And I usually like to surround myself with people who regard my particular views as sound and noteworthy. My only hope is that, as I read this ancient text we call the Bible that I remain open to other interpretations and primarily to the influence of the Holy Spirit.

I have asked God to show me how he has addressed the three issues that I am dealing with right now:

unemployment, disappointment, and waiting. The first entry deals with the view from 10,000 feet. An epiphany, if you will, of my last 8 years. The subsequent entries examine the Scriptures using study practices I learned in seminary and then drawing conclusions that we can apply to our lives.

***"All Bible passages are taken from the New International Version unless otherwise noted.**

# Introduction
# "The Expendable Crewman"

I am a huge fan of the 1960s Star Trek series. There were 79 episodes and most of them had at least one expendable crewman. We all know Captain Kirk, Spock, McCoy and Scotty, but who were those guys in the red shirts? To begin an episode, the Enterprise would establish an orbit around a planet, because there was some suspicious activity down below. Then the main characters would beam down with a compliment of other guys . . . the guys in the red shirts. They were either security or extra explorers, and Kirk would send them to go investigate some noise or puff of smoke. Sure enough, one or more of them would get killed. We rarely knew the name of this crewman and no one seemed particularly broken up about it. The remaining crew would use their phasers to bury them in a rock or pile rocks on top of them, and then the mission would continue. By the end of the show, Kirk, Spock, and McCoy would be cracking jokes and everything was resolved . . . except for the expendable crewman.

During these last eight years without a pastoral position, I have wondered if God works like Star Trek episodes. Does He have main actors . . . and then all the rest of us? Are the plans of the universe going on without me as I struggle to find employment, support my family, and find meaning for my existence? I began to think of myself as an "expendable crewman." This book wrestles honestly with issues that come up when dealing with unemployment, waiting on God to answer desperate prayers, and wondering if we have real significance.

# Why 40 days?

Because God considers 40 days a spiritually significant time period. Whenever he wanted to prepare someone for his purposes, he took 40 days to do it.

- Noah was transformed by 40 days of rain.
  Genesis 6-9
- Moses was changed by 40 days on Mount Sinai.
  Exodus 24 & 34
- The spies were transformed by 40 days in the Promised Land.
  Numbers 13
- David was equipped by Goliath's 40-day challenge.
  1 Samuel 17
- Elijah was transformed when God gave him 40 days of strength from a single meal.
  1 Kings 19
- The people of Nineveh repented when God gave them 40 days to choose.
  Jonah 3

- Jesus was empowered for ministry by 40 days in the wilderness.
  Matthew 4
- The disciples were transformed by 40 days with Jesus after his resurrection.
  Acts 1

I hope you will be encouraged and challenged to consider what God has to say right where you are now. May the examples of men and women in the Bible cause you to consider the impact you can have in this world, no matter what you are experiencing.

Note: White space has been intentionally left so that you can take notes and record your insights.

# Table of Contents

| | | |
|---|---|---|
| Day 1 | What is This Thing............................11 Psalm 142 | |
| Day 2 | Adam and Eve Get Fired.....................15 Genesis 2:22-3:24 | |
| Day 3 | Cain and Abel: Right Product/ Wrong Time.........................................21 Genesis 4:1-12 | |
| Day 4 | Noah's New Career............................27 Genesis 6:1-8 | |
| Day 5 | The Tower of Babel: Poor Vision and Even Worse Strategy...................31 Genesis 11:1-9 | |
| Day 6 | Abram and Sarai: Are We There Yet?....................................35 Genesis 12:1-20 | |
| Day 7 | Abram and Sarai: He Has My Job, What Do I Do?..........................40 Genesis 15:1-20 | |
| Day 8 | Would I Have Been Chosen?..............45 Matthew 4:18-22 | |
| Day 9 | The Good Life...................................49 Matthew 5:1-12 | |
| Day 10 | Jacob and Esau: Short Term Gain Over Long Term Loss..................54 Genesis 25:12-34 | |
| Day 11 | Joseph Part 1: A Career Ending Episode...............................59 Genesis 37 | |
| Day 12 | Joseph: Part 2: Rise to Fame..............64 Genesis 39-41 | |
| Day 13 | Joseph: Part 3: Family Reunion..........70 Genesis 42-45 | |
| Day 14 | Avodah: Work and Worship................76 Exodus 35 | |

| | | |
|---|---|---|
| Day 15 | Moses' Objections and Ours............82 | |
| | Exodus 3 and 4 | |
| Day 16 | Joshua: Military Leader and Aide to Moses...............................90 | |
| | Exodus 17, 24; Numbers 14 | |
| Day 17 | Joshua: Leader of Israel..................95 | |
| | Joshua 24:1-26 | |
| Day 18 | Deborah: Prophetess, Judge and Team-Player..........................101 | |
| | Judges 4 | |
| Day 19 | Actions of the Wise......................106 | |
| | Matthew 2:1-18 | |
| Day 20 | Trumpets and Broken Jars: God's Instruments of Salvation....................................112 | |
| | Judges 6 & 7 | |
| Day 21 | Jephthah: Mighty Warrior and Mighty Fool............................118 | |
| | Judges 11 | |
| Day 22 | John the Baptist: Entrepreneur........123 and Rabble Rouser | |
| | Matthew 3:1-12 | |
| Day 23 | Ruth: A Woman of Character..........128 | |
| | Ruth 1-4 | |
| Day 24 | Jesus: Would you invite Him to Your Company Party?...............135 | |
| | John 2:1-12 | |
| Day 25 | Jesus: The Ideal Boss...................139 | |
| | Mark 10:17-31 | |
| Day 26 | Jesus: The Ideal Employee............146 | |
| | Luke 9:21-27 | |
| Day 27 | Jesus: Company Policy................150 | |
| | John 3:1-21 | |
| Day 28 | Jesus: Equal Pay for Equal Work....................................156 | |
| | John 4 | |

| | | |
|---|---|---|
| Day 29 | Jesus: Understanding the Mission....162<br>John 6:16-30 | |
| Day 30 | Jesus: Fulfillment of the Contract:<br>Part 1............................................168<br>John 6:25-59 | |
| Day 31 | Jesus: Fulfillment of the Contract:<br>Part 2............................................174<br>John 6:60-71 | |
| Day 32 | Jesus: True Bearing.........................178<br>John 8:1-11 | |
| Day 33 | Hannah: A Righteous Woman in<br>Sinful Times...................................183<br>1 Samuel 1:1-17 | |
| Day 34 | My Employer is a Son of the Devil.....189<br>1 Samuel 2:12-36 | |
| Day 35 | Waiting? Unemployed? The Time<br>is Right..........................................196<br>1 Samuel 3:1-20 | |
| Day 36 | Be Careful What You Ask For............202<br>1 Samuel 8:1-10:1 | |
| Day 37 | Religion and Politics:<br>Necessary Collaboration..................208<br>1 Samuel 12:1-25 | |
| Day 38 | Saul: Privileged Position/<br>Poor Attitude..................................214<br>1 Samuel 13:1-15 | |
| Day 39 | Making a New Start.........................220<br>1 Samuel 16:1-13 | |
| Day 40 | Rejected by Jesus..........................225<br>Mark 5:1-20<br>Epilogue........................................231 | |

# Day 1

We Begin with God's Word

Psalm 142

*I cry aloud to the Lord;*
*I lift up my voice to the Lord for mercy.*
*I pour out before him my complaint;*
*before him I tell my trouble.*
*When my spirit grows faint within me,*
*it is you who watch over my way.*
*In the path where I walk*
*people have hidden a snare for me.*
*Look and see, there is no one at my right hand;*
*no one is concerned for me.*
*I have no refuge;*
*no one cares for my life.*
*I cry to you, Lord;*
*I say, "You are my refuge,*
*my portion in the land of the living."*
*Listen to my cry,*
*for I am in desperate need;*
*rescue me from those who pursue me,*
*for they are too strong for me.*
*Set me free from my prison,*
*that I may praise your name.*
*Then the righteous will gather about me*
*because of your goodness to me.*

# What is This That You Have Given Me?

For eight years I have examined my past, I have studied the Scriptures, I have consulted with godly men and women, and I have cried out to God for wisdom and understanding. Up to 2011 when I interviewed for a job, I got it. Ministries grew, people expressed appreciation and God confirmed my calling as a pastor even when some would seek to undermine my efforts. But for the past eight years I have felt like I have been living in an alternate universe. Where things do not go according to plan and I can hardly get an interview much less a job.

Am I alone in this experience? Is everyone else successful while I slip into oblivion? Or could I be asking the wrong questions. Maybe there's a perspective that I haven't considered.

David wrote Psalm 142 about a time when he was hiding from King Saul in a cave. He had been anointed by Samuel years earlier as God's chosen man to be King over Israel. God had given him success over Goliath and many of his enemies. But now....where are the victories? Where is the intimacy he once had with his people and with God? Like everyone, he had sinned but he knew God had forgiven him. Ah, but there are always those pesky consequences. He even cries out, *"No one is concerned for me. I have no refuge; no one is concerned for my life."* That's the cry of a lonely and desperate man. It is our cry too. I've heard it. I've said it myself.

Could it be that the place where we find ourselves is *intended* by God? Wait a minute! *'I thought God wanted only good for me. I thought God was our ABBA father....our Daddy.'* "*What father when a son asks for a fish gives him a snake*" (Matthew 7:10)? For eight years I have identified with Esau when he begged his father, Isaac for a blessing, *"Is there anything left for me"* (Genesis 27:36)? Have I been left out or overlooked? Did I miss class on the day they were handing out blessings?

The loss of a job, an illness, a wayward child, the death of a loved one, or any other tragedy leads us to ask: Where are you God? What did I do to deserve this? Just like David did in Psalm 142.

But what if we reframe our experience, see it from a different angle? David goes on to recall something he'd temporarily forgotten. *"You are my refuge, my portion in the land of the living."*

I attended a conference, where I had gone to recharge my batteries and hopefully be inspired, the speaker gave us this question to mull over:

### "What is this that you have given me?"

The word "given" infers a gift. And if God is good then doesn't it make sense that everything that comes from him is good as well? So, could it be that my job loss is some kind of gift? What about my sciatic pain, or anything else that a normal person would interpret as a tragedy? If "this thing" is from God then I have hope, and I have purpose! I still have to fight feelings of abandonment and emotions that threaten to tear me apart, but I can return to Psalm 142, *"When my spirit grows faint within me, it is you who watch over my way."*

What if God's goal for my life is not a successful career by the world's standard?  What if God's purposes for me are contrary to everything I have believed up to this point?  Can I really say with the Psalmist, *"Better is one day in your courts than a thousand elsewhere. I would rather be a doorkeeper in the house of God than dwell in the tents of the wicked"* (Psalm 84:10)?

What values keep you afloat?  Will you continue to bang your head against the wall determined to believe that your way is right?  Or surrender?  I'm scared but I'm excited too. Has God been waiting for me to catch on and do things his way?  As I read back over the previous paragraphs, I have asked a lot of questions. Where are you going to find your answers?

Application:
1. What reasons have you come up with as to why you are in your current predicament?
2. How might your situation actually be a blessing?
3. From where do you get your philosophy of life?
4. What risks are there to changing your current perspective? What if you've been wrong?
5. What will you do if your definition of "success" needs to change?

\*     \*     \*

*"You can't possibly master enough principles and disciplines to ensure that your life works out. You weren't meant to, and God won't let you. For He knows that if we succeed without him, we will be infinitely further from Him. We will come to believe terrible things about the universe - things like - I can make it on my own and if I only try harder, I can succeed. "*
John Eldredge, Walking with God

# Day 2

We Begin with God's Word

Genesis 2:22-3:24

*Then the Lord God made a woman from the rib he had taken out of the man, and he brought her to the man. The man said, "This is now bone of my bones and flesh of my flesh; she shall be called 'woman,' for she was taken out of man." That is why a man leaves his father and mother and is united to his wife, and they become one flesh. Adam and his wife were both naked, and they felt no shame.*

*Now the serpent was more crafty than any of the wild animals the Lord God had made. He said to the woman, "Did God really say, 'You must not eat from any tree in the garden'?" The woman said to the serpent, "We may eat fruit from the trees in the garden, but God did say, 'You must not eat fruit from the tree that is in the middle of the garden, and you must not touch it, or you will die.'"*

*"You will not certainly die," the serpent said to the woman. "For God knows that when you eat from it your eyes will be opened, and you will be like God, knowing good and evil." When the woman saw that the fruit of the tree was good for food and pleasing to the eye, and also desirable for gaining wisdom, she took some and ate it. She also gave some to her husband, who was with her, and he ate it. Then the eyes of both of them were opened, and they realized they were naked; so they sewed fig leaves together and made coverings for themselves.*

*Then the man and his wife heard the sound of the Lord God as he was walking in the garden in the cool of the day, and they hid from the Lord God among the trees of the garden. But the Lord God called to the man, "Where are you?" He answered, "I heard you in the garden, and I was afraid because I was naked; so I hid."*

*And he said, "Who told you that you were naked? Have you eaten from the tree that I commanded you not to eat from?" The man said, "The woman you put here with me—she gave me some fruit from the tree, and I ate it." Then the Lord God said to the woman, "What is this you have done?" The woman said, "The serpent deceived me, and I ate." So the Lord God said to the serpent, "Because you have done this, "Cursed are you above all livestock and all wild animals! You will crawl on your belly and you will eat dust all the days of your life. And I will put enmity between you and the woman, and between your offspring and hers; he will crush your head, and you will strike his heel." To the woman he said, "I will make your pains in childbearing very severe; with painful labor you will give birth to children. Your desire will be for your husband, and he will rule over you."*

*To Adam he said, "Because you listened to your wife and ate fruit from the tree about which I commanded you, 'You must not eat from it,' "Cursed is the ground because of you; through painful toil you will eat food from it all the days of your life. It will produce thorns and thistles for you, and you will eat the plants of the field. By the sweat of your brow you will eat your food until you return to the ground, since from it you were taken; for dust you are and to dust you will return."*

*Adam named his wife Eve, because she would become the mother of all the living. The Lord God made garments of skin for Adam and his wife and clothed them. And the Lord God said, "The man has now become like one of us, knowing good and evil. He must not be allowed to reach out his hand and take also from the tree of life and eat, and live forever." So the Lord God banished him from the Garden of Eden to work the ground from which he had been taken. After he drove the man out, he placed on the east side of the Garden of Eden cherubim and a flaming sword flashing back and forth to guard the way to the tree of life.*

# Adam and Eve Get Fired

Adam and Eve had jobs.  They were gardeners.  We don't know how hard it was or if they got dirt under their fingernails, but we do know they 'worked'.  They worked because God worked.  Work was intended to be good.  Human beings were designed with this in mind.  But like anything, there were choices to be made.  It appears that God was not a micromanager because he delegated the work of the garden to Adam and Eve.  And it seems Eve had her chores and Adam had his because the instance we discover in Genesis 3 is a time when Eve may have been alone.  An opportune time for Satan, a real being, apparently disguised as a snake, to approach Eve.  Isn't this often the way it is….we get in the most trouble when we are alone?

The result of Eve listening to the serpent and Adam listening to Eve causes a disturbance in the universe.  When it was time for Adam to have his daily meeting with God, he was noticeably absent.  Adam knows he has made a bad choice and doesn't know how to deal with it, so he hides.  Once discovered, he does not confess and ask for forgiveness, he blames God. *"The woman you put here with me—she gave me some fruit from the tree, and I ate it."*  And Eve consequently blames Satan.  Not much has changed.

Is the husband and wife gardening business ruined?  Should they file for bankruptcy?  Is there any hope?  Are there any contingency plans?  Didn't God know this was going to happen?  See what happens when you delegate?

But there is a plan. Genesis 3:14,15 says, *"So the Lord God said to the serpent, "Because you have done this, "Cursed are you above all livestock and all wild animals! You will crawl on your belly and you will eat dust all the days of your life. And I will put enmity between you and the woman, and between your offspring and hers; he will crush your head, and you will strike his heel."* The first prophecy in Scripture. The good news is that God doesn't wait for a confession in order to forgive us. He provides a way to restore people, even before they ask for it.

It's important to note that God's love doesn't remove the consequences for our actions. Eve would now bear children in pain and Adam's work would be frustrating. But, despite the original plan being disrupted, God still provides. The fact that God initiates with love, care and concern separates biblical Christianity from every other world religion.

So, in this time of waiting, unemployment or disappointment what principles can we take away from this passage:
1) We need to stay in community. Remember Eve messed up when Satan got her alone. Find others in the same predicament who can encourage you.
2) God's immediate reaction was to forgive and offer a plan of salvation. Therefore, we should forgive those who have hurt us.
3) Avoid blame and accept the consequences of our actions.
4) We can be encouraged because God is sovereign. His control over the world, over our individual situations and his desire to do us good can give us confidence that our future is in good hands.

From the very beginning God has designed us to work. He delegates the care of the earth to us, allows us to make mistakes, and supplies the resources we need to be redeemed. Facing life knowing how things have been designed enables us to successfully navigate the issues we face on a daily basis.

Application:
1. When was a time when you admitted you made a mistake and took responsibility for it?
2. Who have you had to forgive for hurting you?
3. Do you recognize God's sovereignty and his desire to do you good?

\*     \*     \*

*You see, at just the right time, when we were still powerless, Christ died for the ungodly. Very rarely will anyone die for a righteous person, though for a good person someone might possibly dare to die. But God demonstrates his own love for us in this: While we were still sinners, Christ died for us.*
*(Romans 5:6-8)*

# Day 3

We Begin with God's Word

Genesis 4:1-12

*Adam made love to his wife Eve, and she became pregnant and gave birth to Cain. She said, "With the help of the Lord I have brought forth a man." Later she gave birth to his brother Abel.*

*Now Abel kept flocks, and Cain worked the soil. In the course of time Cain brought some of the fruits of the soil as an offering to the Lord. And Abel also brought an offering—fat portions from some of the firstborn of his flock.*

*The Lord looked with favor on Abel and his offering, but on Cain and his offering he did not look with favor. So Cain was very angry, and his face was downcast. Then the Lord said to Cain, "Why are you angry? Why is your face downcast? If you do what is right, will you not be accepted? But if you do not do what is right, sin is crouching at your door; it desires to have you, but you must rule over it."*

*Now Cain said to his brother Abel, "Let's go out to the field." While they were in the field, Cain attacked his brother Abel and killed him. Then the Lord said to Cain, "Where is your brother Abel?" "I don't know," he replied. "Am I my brother's keeper?" The Lord said, "What have you done? Listen! Your brother's blood cries out to me from the ground. Now you are under a curse and driven from the ground, which opened its mouth to receive your brother's blood from your hand. When you work the ground, it will no longer yield its crops for you. You will be a restless wanderer on the earth."*

## Cain and Abel: Right Product/Wrong Time

In 1940, Henry Ford famously predicted: "Mark my word: a combination airplane and motorcar is coming. You may smile, but it will come." In 1957, Popular Mechanics reported that Hiller Helicopters was developing a ducted-fan aircraft that would be easier to fly than helicopters, and should cost a lot less. Hiller engineers expected that this type of an aircraft would become the basis for a whole family of special-purpose aircraft. And 60 years later, we're still waiting.

Maybe it is the car of the future but the timing has to be right doesn't it? Well, let's go back 6000 years to the first sibling rivalry, Cain and Abel. Two sons who had legitimate occupations marketing legitimate products. Genesis 4 says *"Cain worked the soil"* and *"Abel kept flocks."* They must have traded and benefitted from each other's businesses over the years. But these brothers were born into a world that was distorted and damaged by their parent's disobedience. They didn't know any different, although we imagine Adam and Eve must have told them stories of the garden and what it used to be like in the good 'ole days.

This is the same damaged world into which you and I were born. People, made in the image of God, born with a moral disease...a propensity toward selfishness and rebellion. Cain and Abel must have also grown up regularly sacrificing animals, shedding their blood as a reminder of the seriousness of their sins. Animal sacrifice was a precursor to the perfect and final blood sacrifice of our Savior Jesus Christ. What an image: Adam and Eve, the ones responsible for introducing sin into the world, shedding the blood of an unblemished lamb as a reminder of their sin and a sign that God's love covers their guilt.

When it comes time for the boys to bring offerings for their sin, Cain must have thought that a few things from the field in which he had been working by the sweat of his brow, were surely worthy of an offering to God. Completely ignoring what he had learned from his parents...that a blood sacrifice was required for the forgiveness of sins. Hebrews 9:22 tells us, *"In fact, the law requires that nearly everything be cleansed with blood, and without the shedding of blood there is no forgiveness."*

The result is that God rejects Cain's sacrifice and gives him a chance to correct his mistake. Genesis 4:7 says, *"If you do what is right, will you not be accepted?"* And then this terrible warning, *"But if you do not do what is right, sin is crouching at your door; it desires to have you, but you must rule over it."*

A blood sacrifice was required. No amount of whining, cajoling, manipulation or self-justification is going to change God's mind. But Cain would have none of it. James, the brother of Jesus wrote about this 4000 years later in the New Testament, *"...but each person is tempted when they are dragged away by their own evil desire and enticed. Then, after desire has conceived, it gives birth to sin; and sin, when it is full-grown, gives birth to death"* (James 1:14,15).

So Cain commits the first murder. Abel, who had done nothing to offend Cain, is killed by his jealous brother. God punishes Cain by cursing the ground again and forces him to wander the earth. He whines to God that he is afraid but even here God affirms his love for this selfish murderer by putting a protective mark on him.

Offering the right sacrifice at the right time according to the directives of the Creator was essential to success. We live in a world ordered by this loving creator, but all the same…a world with rules. Some day we might have flying cars but if the timing isn't right, it won't fly…so to speak.

Application:
1. Do the right thing from the beginning. Examine your motives. Recognize the benefit of working with a clear conscience.
2. Avoid jealousy. It leads to foolishness.
3. Deal with your anger - it can make us insane. James 1:20 notes that, *"anger does not make us good."*
4. Avoid self-justification - 'If I murder Abel my problems will be solved.' Or in today's marketplace, "If I cut my workers' salary 40% they'll quit and I won't have to pay their unemployment". It seems like we can convince ourselves of anything when we are desperate and deluded enough.
5. Consider alternative solutions: What could Cain have done instead?
6. Are you living under a curse = Do you have a tainted record, received negative reviews, have you tried to cover-up a deception? Come clean today. As hard as it is, you will be greatly relieved.
7. "Don't burn your bridges" - Our reputation always follows us.
8. Be aware of how easy it is to sin - *"Sin crouches at your door"*. Seek accountability. Take the high road. Look at the long-term affects of your actions rather than acting in the moment.
9. What's your reputation? How do you want to be remembered? Let's learn from Cain's mistake. 1 John 3:12 says, *"Do not be like Cain, who belonged to the evil one and murdered his brother. And why*

*did he murder him? Because his own actions were evil and his brother's were righteous."*

*   *   *

*Commit to the Lord whatever you do, and he will establish your plans.*
(Proverbs 16:3)

# Day 4

We Begin with God's Word

Genesis 6:1-8

*When human beings began to increase in number on the earth and daughters were born to them, the sons of God saw that the daughters of humans were beautiful, and they married any of them they chose. Then the Lord said, "My Spirit will not contend with humans forever, for they are mortal; their days will be a hundred and twenty years."*

*The Nephilim were on the earth in those days—and also afterward—when the sons of God went to the daughters of humans and had children by them. They were the heroes of old, men of renown.*

*The Lord saw how great the wickedness of the human race had become on the earth, and that every inclination of the thoughts of the human heart was only evil all the time. The Lord regretted that he had made human beings on the earth, and his heart was deeply troubled. So the Lord said, "I will wipe from the face of the earth the human race I have created—and with them the animals, the birds and the creatures that move along the ground—for I regret that I have made them." But Noah found favor in the eyes of the Lord*

## Noah's New Career

Genesis 5:32 says, *"At the age of 500 Noah had three sons, Shem, Ham and Japheth."* Five hundred years is a long time. Five hundred years ago our ancestors were either in Europe or Africa, living under the light of candles or campfires. Plumbing was rare and electricity nonexistent. Transportation was mainly on foot or if you were wealthy, by horse. We don't know what technology was available to Noah, but we can assume that the economy was primarily agrarian. One can imagine that in that amount of time, Noah probably acquired many skills that were required to live. There was little use for "knowledge workers". Any expertise you had, better be for starting fires, capturing game, growing food or building homes.

At the age of 500 God commanded Noah to build an ark. A what? That's right, an extremely large boat. In today's measurements: 510 feet long, 50 feet high and 75 feet wide. And where was the boat to be built? In the desert. Whatever Noah and his sons had been doing up to this point, their new career would be boat building. Of course, they couldn't stop growing food or herding animals because these were necessary for living. The immensity of the project begins to sink in for us when we read in Genesis 7:6 that *"Noah was six hundred years old when the floodwaters came on the earth."* That means it took Noah at least 100 years to build the ark.

So many questions come to mind. What did the neighbors think? Genesis 6:9-11 says, *"Noah was a righteous man, blameless among the people of his time, and he walked faithfully with God"* while he rest of the world was called wicked. In essence his behavior was at odds with his community. How did he explain 'boat building' to a desert community? And if he did bother to explain it to them, how would he explain God, the impending rain and God's explanation for the destruction of the world. What would it look like to round up two animals of every kind and the food to feed them? Lastly, didn't anyone in one hundred years change their mind and come to accept Noah's world view? It appears not, because only Noah and his family entered the ark.

Many of us are in our "mature" years and like Noah, are put on edge when asked to think differently about how we should spend our day. Taking on new tasks and training in order to venture into the unknown can be frightening. God patiently waited while the massive vessel was being built but all along the way, Noah must have questioned his own sanity. And his sons, did they hear God's voice like Noah? Aren't family members the toughest people to convince when you have a new idea? What about Noah's wife? We desperately need our spouse's approval. Without it, our homes become very lonely.

This story that's about 5,000 years old is useful even to us today. What timeless principles lie within it?

Application:
1. Be a person of integrity. Who are you when no one is looking?
2. Are you performing the tasks before you to the best of your ability?
3. Who is part of your support network, who believes in you and challenges you?
4. Are you willing to retrain for a new occupation? What would that entail?
5. How do you handle rejection and restructuring?

Noah is remembered as a faithful man. Several times it says that he "obeyed God". He was more concerned with obedience than reputation. What is our reputation right now? What do we want to be remembered for? May we follow Noah's example.

*   *   *

*"By faith Noah, when warned about things not yet seen, in holy fear built an ark to save his family. By his faith he condemned the world and became heir of the righteousness that is in keeping with faith."*
(Hebrews 11:7)

# Day 5

We Begin with God's Word

Genesis 11:1-9

*Now the whole world had one language and a common speech. As people moved eastward, they found a plain in Shinar and settled there. They said to each other, "Come, let's make bricks and bake them thoroughly." They used brick instead of stone, and tar for mortar.*

*Then they said, "Come, let us build ourselves a city, with a tower that reaches to the heavens, so that we may make a name for ourselves; otherwise we will be scattered over the face of the whole earth."*

*But the Lord came down to see the city and the tower the people were building. The Lord said, "If as one people speaking the same language they have begun to do this, then nothing they plan to do will be impossible for them. Come, let us go down and confuse their language so they will not understand each other."*

*So the Lord scattered them from there over all the earth, and they stopped building the city. That is why it was called Babel—because there the Lord confused the language of the whole world. From there the Lord scattered them over the face of the whole earth.*

# The Tower of Babel: Poor Vision and Even Worse Strategy

I am fascinated with beginnings. The opening minutes of a movie can be so intriguing and frustrating because the director is formulating the characters, developing the plot and creating scenes that seem impossibly disparate from one another. We must resist the urge to give into the confusion and jump to another, more simplistic drama or worst of all....start talking to the other people in the room by saying, *"I don't get it. Who's that? What does that character have to do with anything?"*

But movies, as fun as they are, can only mimic real life. Ever heard someone say after seeing an amazing human interest story, *"You can't make this stuff up!"*? Reading the Bible is a bit like watching a good movie. As we read, we discover how complex the human equation is, especially as we come in contact with the God of the universe. The "Tower of Babel" account in Genesis 11 describes our history as a time when people had seemingly forgotten who they were. As I recently heard someone say, we are not *homo sapiens* ("one who is wise" meaning, as a result of evolution we are the only homo species left), but rather we are *homo adoratus* ("one who worships"). As our Bible passage illustrates, when left to our own devices, we tend to worship ourselves and not God. We are made to worship God.

Following Noah, God had commanded the people to multiply and replenish the earth. The people of Babel decided instead that it was safer to settle in one place so as not to be divided. They took it upon themselves to redefine their mission. And they chose to build a tower that showed how great they were . . . using inferior materials. Bricks instead of stone and tar instead of mortar. These materials seemed more readily available and therefore made "common sense."

The story tells us that God, their Creator/supervisor came down to see what they were doing. He determined that due to their lack of wisdom (not sapien-like at all) and their self-centered tendencies, they needed to have their work stopped. Thus, the origin of our multiple languages. Sure, they were unified, accomplishing a great task that only would have been possible through cooperation. But unity at immeasurable cost. Obedience to the mission should have been their primary concern, not unity of the workers.

God intervenes, again, scattering them throughout the earth, so that they can accomplish what had been intended from the beginning. Our world becomes what God intended when it is filled with people who worship him. If we have been in the workforce any time at all we will be able to identify with the transferable principles that Genesis 11 offers.

Application:
1. When we forget our mission we become misguided. Obedience to the mission is primary, not unity of the workers.
2. We need to plan for the future. The people of Babel were only thinking of the NOW and not the ramifications of their impact on future generations.
3. Building with cheaper materials (principles) will be revealed in time and difficulty. Trying to avoid trouble or work by going about something unethically or illegally only makes things worse.

4. Follow the Owner's instructions; don't do things your own way. Without the Owner's permission, we do not have the right to make our own plans.
5. Our work should benefit the company as a whole and not one individual.
6. Seeking to make our own name great often results in being forgotten. We typically remember those who benefit society as a whole rather than just themselves.
7. God checks in on His workers to make sure they are on task, and so does a good boss.
8. God was not a micromanager. The Scripture said, "He came down". He allows us to choose our own way.
9. A good Boss, often times for the greater good, makes demands of the employees that in the short run may feel detrimental, but the long range vision is what benefits everyone.
10. A good Boss is patient but is not afraid to discipline.

We may think we are getting away with our tower of bricks and tar but there will be a final reckoning. Let us examine what we think we are accomplishing today and choose to exercise eternal principles which will not only benefit ourselves, but others as well and we will be fulfilling our calling as homo adoratus.

*   *   *

*"When he finally arrives, blazing in beauty and all his angels with him, the Son of Man will take his place on his glorious throne. Then all the nations will be arranged before him and he will sort the people out, much as a shepherd sorts out sheep and goats, putting sheep to his right and goats to his left."*
(Matthew 25:31,32)

# Day 6

We Begin with God's Word

Genesis 12:1-20

*The Lord had said to Abram, "Go from your country, your people and your father's household to the land I will show you. "I will make you into a great nation, and I will bless you; I will make your name great, and you will be a blessing. I will bless those who bless you, and whoever curses you I will curse; and all peoples on earth will be blessed through you."*

*So Abram went, as the Lord had told him; and Lot went with him. Abram was seventy-five years old when he set out from Harran. He took his wife Sarai, his nephew Lot, all the possessions they had accumulated and the people they had acquired in Harran, and they set out for the land of Canaan, and they arrived there. Abram traveled through the land as far as the site of the great tree of Moreh at Shechem. At that time the Canaanites were in the land. The Lord appeared to Abram and said, "To your offspring I will give this land." So he built an altar there to the Lord, who had appeared to him.*

*From there he went on toward the hills east of Bethel and pitched his tent, with Bethel on the west and Ai on the east. There he built an altar to the Lord and called on the name of the Lord. Then Abram set out and continued toward the Negev. Now there was a famine in the land, and Abram went down to Egypt to live there for a while because the famine was severe. As he was about to enter Egypt, he said to his wife Sarai, "I know what a beautiful woman you are. When the Egyptians see you, they will say, 'This is his wife.' Then they will kill me but will let you live. Say you are my sister, so that I will be treated well for your sake and my life will be spared because of you."*

*When Abram came to Egypt, the Egyptians saw that Sarai was a very beautiful woman. And when Pharaoh's officials saw her, they praised her to Pharaoh, and she was taken into his palace. He treated Abram well for her sake, and Abram acquired sheep and cattle, male and female donkeys, male and female servants, and camels. But the Lord inflicted serious diseases on Pharaoh and his household because of Abram's wife Sarai. So Pharaoh summoned Abram. "What have you done to me?" he said. "Why didn't you tell me she was your wife? Why did you say, 'She is my sister,' so that I took her to be my wife? Now then, here is your wife. Take her and go!" Then Pharaoh gave orders about Abram to his men, and they sent him on his way, with his wife and everything he had.*

## Abram and Sarai: Are We There Yet?

At one time or another, I have made the following excuses: *"I can't get my foot in the door." "Ageism is alive and well." "They keep hiring people with more degrees than me." "Their vision is short-sighted; I could offer so much to them."* Can you identify with any of these as explanations as to why you haven't gotten the job that you wanted? What they amount to are examples of blame, whining and pride. Also, as a follower of Jesus Christ, I am completely forgetting that God is sovereign and He is working his plan out in my life.

In Genesis 12 we read the story of Abram (his name means "high father") and how God spoke to him out of the blue, telling him to move to an undesignated location. At 75 years old, he had many legitimate excuses for not going. And there were some incongruencies in the revelation that, as his neighbor, I might have raised: *"You're too old", "How can you be a "great nation" when you don't have any children, despite the meaning of your name?" "What about your father and your aging wife, they need you to stay here."*

Somehow, Abram saw beyond the excuses and objections. According to the writer of Hebrews, *"He was looking forward to the city with foundations, whose architect and builder is God."* He took the first step and left the land of his fathers and entered "the promised land" only to find it occupied. But God reiterated his promise *"I will give this land to your children."* So much faith was required; a land that is occupied and children to a couple well beyond child-bearing years.

In the world of unemployment, disappointment and waiting our faith is often tested in similar ways. We wonder if our age is a factor. We second-guess our skills and knowledge. We may think that we're the only one going through this and we feel sorry for ourselves.

For Abram, the testing had only just begun. He certainly wasn't fully prepared for what he would experience and he made a lot of mistakes. I am encouraged that the writer of Genesis doesn't hide the fact that Abram and Sarai consorted to deceive Pharaoh by lying about their relationship. Isn't it encouraging that who we now know as a great man of faith, made some stupid mistakes? But I also recognize that there are always consequences to our decisions. Abram's deception hurt Pharaoh and his kingdom.

It's good to recognize that our decisions do not happen in a vacuum. Abram learned from his mistakes, was forgiven and went on to be remembered as a man of God. May we do the same.

Application:
1. Just as God tested Abram's loyalty by giving him a monumental mission, there comes a time when your employer will test your loyalty by giving you more responsibility. How can you plan now to be ready to say "yes"?
2. When is the right time to leave a job? Following a layoff I've often heard people say, "Losing my job was the best thing that ever happened to me." Abram was called to leave his home for a new adventure. Are you faced with a similar choice?
3. What excuses do you use about your present circumstances? What do you see as barriers to making changes or getting a new job?

4. Have you ever stayed in a job that failed the integrity test because you were afraid about financial insecurity?
5. Have you envisioned your job as not just about yourself but so that you might be a blessing to others?
6. How have your ethical and moral choices at work affected others?
7. When your boss has reprimanded you for doing something wrong, how have you handled it?
8. How have you and other followers of Christ integrated your faith into your work life?
9. Since no job is permanent, where do you get your sense of true security?
10. If you find yourself unable to make a change, it could be you are more concerned to please people than obey God. If you imagine whole-heartedly trusting God, where would he lead you now?

\* \* \*

*By faith Abraham, when called to go to a place he would later receive as his inheritance, obeyed and went, even though he did not know where he was going. By faith he made his home in the promised land like a stranger in a foreign country; he lived in tents, as did Isaac and Jacob, who were heirs with him of the same promise. For he was looking forward to the city with foundations, whose architect and builder is God.*

(Hebrews 11:8-10)

# Day 7

We Begin with God's Word

Genesis 15:1-20

*The word of the Lord came to Abram in a vision: "Do not be afraid, Abram. I am your shield, your very great reward." But Abram said, "Sovereign Lord, what can you give me since I remain childless and the one who will inherit my estate is Eliezer of Damascus?" And Abram said, "You have given me no children; so a servant in my household will be my heir." Then the word of the Lord came to him: "This man will not be your heir, but a son who is your own flesh and blood will be your heir." He took him outside and said, "Look up at the sky and count the stars—if indeed you can count them." Then he said to him, "So shall your offspring be."*

*Abram believed the Lord, and he credited it to him as righteousness. He also said to him, "I am the Lord, who brought you out of Ur of the Chaldeans to give you this land to take possession of it." But Abram said, "Sovereign Lord, how can I know that I will gain possession of it?" So the Lord said to him, "Bring me a heifer, a goat and a ram, each three years old, along with a dove and a young pigeon. Abram brought all these to him, cut them in two and arranged the halves opposite each other; the birds, however, he did not cut in half. Then birds of prey came down on the carcasses, but Abram drove them away.*

*As the sun was setting, Abram fell into a deep sleep, and a thick and dreadful darkness came over him. Then the Lord said to him, "Know for certain that for four hundred years your descendants will be strangers in a country not their own and that they will be enslaved and mistreated there. But I will punish the nation they serve as slaves, and afterward they will come out with great possessions. You, however, will go to your ancestors in peace and be buried at a good old age. In the fourth generation your descendants will come back here, for the sin of the Amorites has not yet reached its full measure."*

*When the sun had set and darkness had fallen, a smoking fire pot with a blazing torch appeared and passed between the pieces. On that day the Lord made a covenant with Abram and said, "To your descendants I give this land, from the Wadi of Egypt to the great river, the Euphrates - the land of the Kenites, Kenizzites, Kadmonites, Hittites, Perizzites, Rephaites...*

# Abram and Sarai:
# He Has My job, What Do I Do?

One morning at Career Prospectors we talked about the Hidden Network of the job search. The job that we often want is not advertised, or someone else already has it. In ancient kingdoms the strategy was to bump off the king in order to take his place, but I suppose that's not an option today. The Bible tells us that we each have God-given gifts and abilities, so we can find jobs where we can flourish and be valuable, contributing members to society.

Abram and Sarai had been promised by God that their descendants would inhabit the land of Canaan. At ages 75 and 65 they had left all they had known to go to an unknown land. By the time we get to Genesis 15 Abram is in his early 80's and God's promise of a descendant has not been fulfilled. Abram complains that, after waiting for years, it appears that his servant will be his heir. God reaffirms that, indeed, it will not be so, but, *"a son who is your own flesh and blood will be your heir."*

Abram has a moment of clarity and accepts this truth. Unfortunately, his confidence doesn't last long because he questions God's promise regarding taking possession of the land. Aren't we like that as well? One moment we have the confidence to take on the world, the next we don't have the strength to get out of bed. We are a fickle people.

What kind of promises are these? Two seemingly impossible things: to have a child in old age, and to inhabit an already inhabited land. The job search is fraught with fear and doubt. When we find a job we love, we may discover that someone already has it. When we interview we may experience discrimination albeit ever so subtle. We may say with Abram, *"Sovereign Lord, how can I know that I will gain possession of it?"*

As God was with Abram, so he will be with us. God put up with Abram's fear and doubt and provided a demonstration. In this Bible passage God performs what the ancients knew as the Suzerain treaty, a covenant between two unequal parties. Animals were cut in two and laid apart with a path in between. The weaker of the kingdoms would walk between the animals and say, "If I ever break this treaty, may the same happen to me as happened to these animals." But in this instance Abram (the weaker party) prepares the animals and then waits. I have experienced this as well. I feel confident that God is leading me only to have to wait some more.

But then something amazing happens. Abram falls into a deep sleep and a smoking pot passes between the animals. What happened?!? It appears that the smoking pot, representing God himself, passes through the sacrificed animals. Thus God is saying, "If I ever do not fulfill my promise to you, may this happen to me." This is something a powerful kingdom or ruler would never do, but this is the God we worship. A God who sacrifices himself in order to save the people he loves.

Application:
1) Abram learned that the reward for obedience wasn't necessarily the promised heir or even the promised land, but God himself. Too often we put our focus on that elusive job or what we imagine as

what we need and we miss a relationship with our Creator.
2) Waiting has tremendous value. What can we learn from having to wait for what we want?
3) We appreciate the end result of the promise more when we have experienced the deprivation of exile and punishment. Therefore, unemployment can often produce better employees than steady employment.
4) View your circumstances in light of God's past faithfulness. In periods of uncertainty, we can be certain at least of God.

I'll never forget hearing my Old Testament professor tell us the story of Genesis 15 through the lens of the culture of that day. God used the cultural practice of the Suzerain Treaty to demonstrate how he often reverses misconceptions of himself and even our worldview. Choose today what you will believe: circumstances that appear dire and hopeless or the God who has demonstrated faithfulness in the past and offers hope for the future.

God says this through Jeremiah to a people about to go into seventy years of exile:

\*   \*   \*

*"For I know the plans I have for you," declares the Lord, "plans to prosper you and not to harm you, plans to give you hope and a future."*
(Jeremiah 29:11)

# Day 8

We Begin with God's Word

Matthew 4:18-22

*As Jesus was walking beside the Sea of Galilee, he saw two brothers, Simon called Peter and his brother Andrew. They were casting a net into the lake, for they were fishermen. "Come, follow me," Jesus said, "and I will send you out to fish for people." At once they left their nets and followed him.*

*Going on from there, he saw two other brothers, James son of Zebedee and his brother John. They were in a boat with their father Zebedee, preparing their nets. Jesus called them, and immediately they left the boat and their father and followed him.*

## Would I Have Been Chosen?

Jesus chose his disciples. That doesn't sound so unusual. But 2,000 years ago, potential disciples applied to study under a rabbi hoping to be accepted as their student. Not too different from today's employment picture. Another difference is that the ones Jesus chose - Simon, Peter, Andrew, James and John - were not looking for a career change. They were fishermen, working on the open sea, mending nets, dealing daily with weather and selling their catch to retail merchants.

Jesus used a play on words in order to reel these men in. *"Come, follow me,"* Jesus said, *"and I will send you out to fish for people."* Pretty clever! I wonder if Jesus worked with a branding expert before he went out and tried it on people. Maybe, being a carpenter himself he thought about going after fellow wood workers. *'Come follow me and we'll hammer the truth home'.* Or farmers.... *'Come follow me and plant seeds you can harvest forever.'* Actually, he used that one later on.

The text doesn't say whether these men struggled with their decision, if James and John argued with their father, or if there was any deliberation at all. Were they so convinced of Jesus' reputation that they were willing to leave a successful career for one of uncertainty? If so, they were in good company. Abraham left his home at the age of 75. Noah became a carpenter at the age of 500. Prophets spoke God's Word at great risk to their reputation.

If our faith is of primary importance to us, what does that imply regarding our choice of a career? Of course God needs people in all professions, so who will we be while selling widgets, representing insurance or financial institutions or working with our hands? The men Jesus chose must have demonstrated diligence in their current calling for him to trust them with a new one. What is our reputation currently? Are we men and women of integrity who can be trusted with greater responsibility?

I also like the fact that Jesus chose men of common reputation. He didn't go looking for the privileged and educated. Nor did he choose the religious leaders of the day. Wouldn't that have made sense? Aside from the education they got at home, what did these fishermen know about the deeper truths of their faith? The well-educated would have been the better candidates. By reading the Gospels we learn that the teachers of the Law had gotten off message, so much so, that in their quest for the Messiah, they completely missed him when he was standing there in the flesh.

Sometimes we make too much of our experience and education (or lack thereof) when the most important trait is the ability to be teachable. It appears that the fishermen were the best qualified for the job.

Many of my friends are in the market for a new job. Some voluntarily and others by the choice of others. It's an opportune time to examine our lives and not only decide the kind of job we want, but also to determine what kind of people we will be. The topics we talk about in our job-seekers group, Career Prospectors, are not only for the benefit of ourselves but also to the betterment of society. We learn that, when we help others, we become better people.

I can imagine that the customers and even the families of these fishermen were detrimentally affected in the short run by their seemingly rash decision to follow this new rabbi. But long term…OH MY! Because they followed Jesus, the church is the most successful venture in world history. The message of Jesus Christ has gone out into all the world. Their choice that day to stop fishing for tilapia and to take the message of the Messiah to all *homo adoratus* (men and women) radically transformed the world.

Application:
1) What am I doing today to make myself attractive to future employers?
2) What life skills do I have that go beyond simple employability? Examples: 1) I have an uncanny ability to collaborate with others, therefore I have created effective teams. 2) The frequent changes in my career have enabled me to quickly adapt to new circumstances.
3) Those of us who have experienced the challenge of unemployment are even more valuable because our worldview now includes a world previously unknown. (I believe facing adversity successfully makes us better people.)
4) Faith in God will lead us into places that we never imagined. Are you ready to trust him?
5) Are we men and women of integrity who can be trusted with greater responsibility?

\*     \*     \*

*I thank my God every time I remember you. In all my prayers for all of you, I always pray with joy because of your partnership in the gospel from the first day until now, being confident of this, that he who began a good work in you will carry it on to completion until the day of Christ Jesus.*

*(Philippians 1:3-6)*

# Day 9

We Begin with God's Word

Matthew 5:1-12

*Now when Jesus saw the crowds, he went up on a mountainside and sat down. His disciples came to him, and he began to teach them.*

*He said: "Blessed are the poor in spirit, for theirs is the kingdom of heaven. Blessed are those who mourn, for they will be comforted. Blessed are the meek, for they will inherit the earth. Blessed are those who hunger and thirst for righteousness, for they will be filled. Blessed are the merciful, for they will be shown mercy. Blessed are the pure in heart, for they will see God. Blessed are the peacemakers, for they will be called children of God. Blessed are those who are persecuted because of righteousness, for theirs is the kingdom of heaven. Blessed are you when people insult you, persecute you and falsely say all kinds of evil against you because of me. Rejoice and be glad, because great is your reward in heaven, for in the same way they persecuted the prophets who were before you."*

# The Good Life

We all want the good life. Most people would say the good life is about having good health, enough money to pay the bills and have some fun, and close family and friends. But what if these things, as wonderful as they are, are *not* the essence of a truly good life? What if they're actually secondary to what really matters? How would we find out what truly makes up a life that is good? And is there enough time on this planet to discover these things?

There's a reason why Jesus is still relevant today. Even though he lived two thousand years ago, his "visit" affected every human being because he taught about the Good Life. He even showed it, through miracles and his own death and resurrection. In Matthew 5 Jesus delivers what has come to be called "The Beatitudes." These statements shook up the people then and they continue to rattle us today, if we let them.

It's always important, when interpreting a Bible passage, to understand its original context. One important thing to note is that this "Sermon on the Mount," as some call it, was spoken to Jews who were under Roman domination. Most of these people were doing their best to eke out a living the best they could. Some Jews discovered that if they collected taxes from their own people on behalf of Rome they could earn a good income. Matthew was one of these people; he was a tax collector. Another fact to bear in mind is that the Jewish leaders were continually creating new laws to obey, supposedly to make them more holy.

The other important fact to note is it had been 400 years since a prophet had spoken to the people of Israel. That's a very long time.

So, what did Jesus have to say that could challenge the hypocritical and arrogant while comforting the poor and oppressed?

#1     *Blessed are the poor in spirit* - Learn to depend fully upon God, so that nothing of this world causes undue pride nor leads to despair.  The Kingdom of Heaven has come upon this earth, and those who have crossed over from death to life have begun to grasp what this means.  Therefore, unemployment, illness nor wealth and success do not have to detract from the good life.

#2     *Blessed are those who mourn* - The people that I trust the most are those who can identify with my pain.  Our lives of disappointment are most appreciated by others who recognize their own dashed dreams and seek solace in the words of Jesus.

#3     *Blessed are the meek* - To be meek toward others implies freedom from malice and a vengeful spirit.  Are we not attracted to those who build us up, easily forgive and genuinely love others?  And we run from those who suck the life out of us with their arrogance and manipulation.

#4     *Blessed are those who hunger and thirst for righteousness* - Truth and honesty are not always the accepted values.  Short-sighted goals and pragmatism can lead to a life opposite of a person of integrity.

#5     *Blessed are the merciful* - Mercy and grace are at the center of the Christian faith.  It's an other-worldly trait to forgive a guilty person or open our door to one who is suffering and in need. When I am in the presence of such a person, I cannot help but feel cared for and loved.  It's a trait that shows little return on investment but it has the power to change lives.

#6     *Blessed are the pure in heart* - Jesus is saying that it's not just about doing right, it's being made right. Our "heart," our motives and character, have a way of being revealed when we are struggling with life's challenges.  Again, the reward may not be measured in money and influence, but Jesus says we will see God. The ultimate reward.

#7     *Blessed are the peacemakers* -   Angst and turmoil will surround a person that is not at peace. Jesus is the ultimate peacemaker. His death and resurrection brought peace between us and God, if we will accept his path.    I have peace in my job, for example, by working "as if for the Lord" (Colossians 3:23).

#8     *Blessed are those who are persecuted because of righteousness* - Sometimes doing the right thing brings trouble on our heads, but the stories that I've heard from my friends reveal that it also brings peace to our hearts and minds.  Avoiding the opportunity to stand up against wrongs may enable us to avoid persecution but at a high cost, to us and to others.

Jesus demonstrated that His mission was radical but life-giving.  I can imagine being a businessman hearing this message and having to re-evaluate everything. After hearing these words asking,  'Is my definition of "The Good Life" still the same?'

Application:
1. Which of the Beatitudes speaks to your current situation and why?
2. What is your definition of "The Good Life"? How does it need to change, based on what you now know?

\* \* \*

*And as he was setting out on his journey, a man ran up and knelt before him, and asked him, "Good Teacher, what must I do to inherit eternal life?" And Jesus said to him, "Why do you call me good? No one is good but God alone. You know the commandments: 'Do not kill, Do not commit adultery, Do not steal, Do not bear false witness, Do not defraud, Honor your father and mother.'" And he said to him, "Teacher, all these I have observed from my youth." And Jesus looking upon him loved him, and said to him, "You lack one thing; go, sell what you have, and give to the poor, and you will have treasure in heaven; and come, follow me." At that saying his countenance fell, and he went away sorrowful; for he had great possessions.*

(Mark 10:17-22)

# Day 10

We Begin with God's Word

Genesis 25:12-34

*This is the account of the family line of Abraham's son Ishmael, whom Sarah's slave, Hagar the Egyptian, bore to Abraham.*

*These are the names of the sons of Ishmael, listed in the order of their birth: Nebaioth the firstborn of Ishmael, Kedar, Adbeel, Mibsam, Mishma, Dumah, Massa, Hadad, Tema, Jetur, Naphish and Kedemah. These were the sons of Ishmael, and these are the names of the twelve tribal rulers according to their settlements and camps. Ishmael lived a hundred and thirty-seven years. He breathed his last and died, and he was gathered to his people. His descendants settled in the area from Havilah to Shur, near the eastern border of Egypt, as you go toward Ashur. And they lived in hostility toward all the tribes related to them.*

*This is the account of the family line of Abraham's son Isaac. Abraham became the father of Isaac, and Isaac was forty years old when he married Rebekah daughter of Bethuel the Aramean from Paddan Aram and sister of Laban the Aramean.*

*Isaac prayed to the Lord on behalf of his wife, because she was childless. The Lord answered his prayer, and his wife Rebekah became pregnant. The babies jostled each other within her, and she said, "Why is this happening to me?" So she went to inquire of the Lord.*

*The Lord said to her, "Two nations are in your womb,and two peoples from within you will be separated; one people will be stronger than the other, and the older will serve the younger."*

*When the time came for her to give birth, there were twin boys in her womb. The first to come out was red, and his whole body was like a hairy garment; so they named him Esau. After this, his brother came out, with his hand grasping Esau's heel; so he was named Jacob. Isaac was sixty years old when Rebekah gave birth to them.*

*The boys grew up, and Esau became a skillful hunter, a man of the open country, while Jacob was content to stay at home among the tents. Isaac, who had a taste for wild game, loved Esau, but Rebekah loved Jacob. Once when Jacob was cooking some stew, Esau came in from the open country, famished. He said to Jacob, "Quick, let me have some of that red stew! I'm famished!" (That is why he was also called Edom.)*

*Jacob replied, "First sell me your birthright." "Look, I am about to die," Esau said. "What good is the birthright to me?" But Jacob said, "Swear to me first." So he swore an oath to him, selling his birthright to Jacob. Then Jacob gave Esau some bread and some lentil stew. He ate and drank, and then got up and left. So Esau despised his birthright.*

## Jacob and Esau:
## Short-Term Gain Over Long-Term Loss

My brother, Rob, and his wife had twins for their first children. Rob used to ask parents who had only one infant what they did with all their free time. Imagine getting ready for your first child and then the news comes - you have to multiply everything by two! And of course, my friends who had quintuplets....unimagineable! In the story from Genesis 25, Isaac and Rebekah have waited twenty years for their first child. Rebekah was initially barren, a trait shared by her mother-in-law. This becomes one of the first opportunities for the couple to demonstrate their faith. And, like my brother and his wife, Isaac and Rebekah get a double blessing. But also a blessing with a prophecy:

*"Two nations are in your womb, and two peoples from within you will be separated; one people will be stronger than the other, and the older will serve the younger."*

What do you do with such news? We know very little about how the boys grew up, but it seemed that the boys were polar opposites: Esau was an outdoorsman and Jacob preferred to be at home. And their parents showed favoritism so much so the Scripture records: *"Isaac loved Esau and Rebekah loved Jacob."*

We enter the story where Esau has come back from hunting and Jacob is at home cooking. Like a typical adolescent boy, Esau comes home "hungry enough to die". Jacob seems prepared for this moment because he bargains for his brother's birthright as the firstborn.

Quite a coup, since the first-born received an inheritance twice as large as the next in line.

Esau again responds impetuously, *"Look, I am about to die, what good is the birthright to me?"* What are we willing to give up in the long run for a short term prize? From birth, Jacob, whose name means "supplanter", was destined to be ruler over his brother but could the prophecy have been fulfilled without deceit? If we feel we have been overlooked or misrepresented, have we resorted to deceitful means or remained a person of integrity?

This portion of the story concludes with, *"So Esau despised his birthright."* Even if we don't know anything else about the story, we must assume that things probably did not turn out well for Esau. And we must ask, "Did Jacob get away with his deceit?" Do we live our lives with the philosophy that "the end justifies the means"? Questions of honor, virtue and decency should always be in the forefront of our minds.

Application:
1. Rebekah's response to trouble was to pray? What's our first response when things get difficult, and why?
2. Jacob was destined to rule over Esau. Sometimes people are chosen over us for no apparent reason. How do we respond?
3. Favoritism in families is toxic. It is harmful in the workplace as well.
4. Employees should be appreciated for their specific gifts, even though some gifts will be more public than others.

5. Esau and Jacob could have repented of their behavior. What difference would that have made for them and their families?
6. Don't give up a long-term vision for a short-term gain.
7. Have you experienced the qualities of repentance, seeking forgiveness, and granting mercy as honored business practices? Or have you stood up for what is right and are still waiting for the end of the story?

\*　　\*　　\*

*Jesus said, "What good is it for someone to gain the whole world, yet forfeit their soul?"*
*(Mark 8:36)*

# Day 11

We Begin with God's Word

Excerpts from Genesis 37

*This is the account of Jacob's family line. Joseph, a young man of seventeen, was tending the flocks with his brothers, the sons of Bilhah and the sons of Zilpah, his father's wives, and he brought their father a bad report about them. Now Israel loved Joseph more than any of his other sons, because he had been born to him in his old age; and he made an ornate robe for him. When his brothers saw that their father loved him more than any of them, they hated him and could not speak a kind word to him.*

*Joseph had a dream, and when he told it to his brothers, they hated him all the more. He said to them, "Listen to this dream I had: We were binding sheaves of grain out in the field when suddenly my sheaf rose and stood upright, while your sheaves gathered around mine and bowed down to it." His brothers said to him, "Do you intend to reign over us? Will you actually rule us?" And they hated him all the more because of his dream and what he had said.*

*Now his brothers had gone to graze their father's flocks near Shechem, and Israel said to Joseph, "As you know, your brothers are grazing the flocks near Shechem. Come, I am going to send you to them." So Joseph went after his brothers and found them near Dothan. But they saw him in the distance, and before he reached them, they plotted to kill him. "Here comes that dreamer!" they said to each other. "Come now, let's kill him and throw him into one of these cisterns and say that a ferocious animal devoured him. Then we'll see what comes of his dreams."*

*As they sat down to eat their meal, they looked up and saw a caravan of Ishmaelites coming from Gilead. Their camels were loaded with spices, balm and myrrh, and they were on their way to take them down to Egypt. So when the Midianite merchants came by, his brothers pulled Joseph up out of the cistern and sold him for twenty shekels of silver to the Ishmaelites, who took him to Egypt.*

*Then they got Joseph's robe, slaughtered a goat and dipped the robe in the blood. They took the ornate robe back to their father and said, "We found this. Examine it to see whether it is your son's robe." He recognized it and said, "It is my son's robe! Some ferocious animal has devoured him. Joseph has surely been torn to pieces." Then Jacob tore his clothes, put on sackcloth and mourned for his son many days. All his sons and daughters came to comfort him, but he refused to be comforted. "No," he said, "I will continue to mourn until I join my son in the grave." So his father wept for him. Meanwhile, the Midianites sold Joseph in Egypt to Potiphar, one of Pharaoh's officials, the captain of the guard.*

# Joseph Part 1: A Career Ending Episode

Many careers have ended through acts of indiscretion. It seems like every day we hear of another CEO, celebrity, or politician being caught in sexual misconduct, racism, or financial scandal. The young are often guilty of unwise deeds but their behavior reflects their mentors - parents, teachers, coaches who should have helped them make wise choices. As we reflect on the biblical story of Joseph, one has to wonder if his upbringing by his father, Jacob, was not partly to blame for the treatment he received at the hands of his brothers.

Joseph had some unusual dreams, which we, with 20/20 hindsight know their prophetic purpose. At the time they were just dreams, but the way in which he told them infuriated his brothers because Joseph, the favored child, had other behaviors that invigorated his brother's jealousy and ignited their hatred. If they could have just accepted Joseph's narcissism as youthful immaturity maybe they could have just roughed him up a bit and been done with it. Jesus reminds us though, that hate is equivalent to murder. How many times have I wished evil upon someone?

But jealousy, as they say, is like drinking poison and hoping the other person dies. The wonder boy, with dreams of stardom, gets thrown into a pit as the brothers plot his demise. And like any plan with no blueprint, it develops through the philosophy of pragmatism, *whatever seems right at the time*. Ishmaelite traders happen to come along, cousins actually of these brothers, descendants of Abraham. In this land of lawlessness, they sell their brother for a handful of silver. We can imagine Joseph crying out to

God for mercy, bound hand and foot in the wagon of the caravan.

Joseph's brothers, relieved of his whining voice now have to contrive a story to tell their father, which will surely kill him. It becomes a series of deceptions which the brothers must struggle to keep one story between the ten of them straight.

Application:
1) If we are in a period of unemployment, hearing bad news or waiting, we, along with Joseph may be asking, is this it? Am I destined to a downward spiral of debilitating events?
2) What youthful (or recent) indiscretions still haunt you? Can I repent and be released?
3) Do I bear continual hate or resentment toward those who have hurt me? Why am I holding on to it?
4) Have I been slighted or overlooked in my job or even in my family? How should I respond?
5) What evil or wrong have I committed for which I have yet to repent? Even if it was a long time ago, it's good to deal with issues as you remember them. They have a way of resurfacing at inconvenient times.
6) Are you trusting in God's sovereignty to deliver justice while you obey the command of Jesus to respond to evil with good?

\* \* \*

*"Therefore, my dear friends, as you have always obeyed—not only in my presence, but now much more in my absence—continue to work out your salvation with fear and trembling, for it is God who works in*

*you to will and to act in order to fulfill his good purpose."*

*(Philippians 2:12,13)*

# Day 12

We Begin with God's Word

Excerpts from Genesis 39-41

*Now Joseph had been taken down to Egypt. Potiphar, an Egyptian who was one of Pharaoh's officials, the captain of the guard, bought him from the Ishmaelites who had taken him there. The Lord was with Joseph so that he prospered, and he lived in the house of his Egyptian master. When his master saw that the Lord was with him and that the Lord gave him success in everything he did, Joseph found favor in his eyes and became his attendant.*

*Now Joseph was well-built and handsome, and after a while his master's wife took notice of Joseph and said, "Come to bed with me!" But he refused. "With me in charge," he told her, "my master does not concern himself with anything in the house; everything he owns he has entrusted to my care. One day he went into the house to attend to his duties, and none of the household servants was inside. She caught him by his cloak and said, "Come to bed with me!" But he left his cloak in her hand and ran out of the house. Then she laid up his garment by her until his master came home, and she told him the same story, saying, "The Hebrew servant, whom you have brought among us, came in to me to insult me; Joseph's master took him and put him in prison, the place where the king's prisoners were confined.*

*While Joseph was there in the prison, the Lord was with him; he showed him kindness and granted him favor in the eyes of the prison warden. So the warden put Joseph in charge of all those held in the prison, and he was made responsible for all that was done there. When two full years had passed, Pharaoh had a dream: He was standing by the Nile, when out of the river there came up seven cows, sleek and fat, and they grazed among the reeds. After them, seven other cows, ugly and gaunt, came up out of the Nile and stood beside those on the riverbank. And the cows that were ugly and gaunt ate up the seven sleek, fat cows. Then Pharaoh woke up. He fell asleep again and had a second dream: Seven heads of grain, healthy and good, were growing on a single stalk. After them, seven other heads of grain sprouted—thin and scorched by the east wind. The thin heads of grain swallowed up the seven healthy, full heads. Then Pharaoh woke up; it had been a dream.*

*So Pharaoh sent for Joseph, and he was quickly brought from the dungeon. When he had shaved and changed his clothes, he came before Pharaoh. Pharaoh said to Joseph, "I had a dream, and no one can interpret it. But I have heard it said of you that when you hear a dream you can interpret it." "I cannot do it," Joseph replied to Pharaoh, "but God will give Pharaoh the answer he desires."*

*Then Joseph said to Pharaoh, "The dreams of Pharaoh are one and the same. God has revealed to Pharaoh what he is about to do. The seven good cows are seven years, and the seven good heads of grain are seven years; it is one and the same dream. The seven lean, ugly cows that came up afterward are seven years, and so are the seven worthless heads of grain scorched by the east wind: They are seven years of famine.*

So Pharaoh said to Joseph, "I hereby put you in charge of the whole land of Egypt." Then Pharaoh took his signet ring from his finger and put it on Joseph's finger. He dressed him in robes of fine linen and put a gold chain around his neck. He had him ride in a chariot as his second-in-command, and people shouted before him, "Make way!" Thus he put him in charge of the whole land of Egypt.

Joseph collected all the food produced in those seven years of abundance in Egypt and stored it in the cities. In each city he put the food grown in the fields surrounding it. Joseph stored up huge quantities of grain, like the sand of the sea; it was so much that he stopped keeping records because it was beyond measure. There was famine in all the other lands, but in the whole land of Egypt there was food.

When all Egypt began to feel the famine, the people cried to Pharaoh for food. Then Pharaoh told all the Egyptians, "Go to Joseph and do what he tells you." When the famine had spread over the whole country, Joseph opened all the storehouses and sold grain to the Egyptians, for the famine was severe throughout Egypt. And all the world came to Egypt to buy grain from Joseph, because the famine was severe everywhere.

## Joseph Part 2: Rise to Fame

Joseph had been sold as a slave by his brothers. His arrogance and his father's favoritism had been his downfall. The dreams God gave him were misunderstood and what happened during this period reformed Joseph's character.

How did he become the righteous man that we encounter in Potiphar's house? His life as a slave was so exemplary that he rose to prominence in the eyes of everyone who knew him. His character as a righteous man grew in the midst of suffering which enabled him to become Potipar's personal servant and head of household. He wasn't bad looking either. This was something that Mrs. Potiphar took notice of and sought to seduce him. It seems that even though this was something Joseph could have gotten away with, he resisted because it would have been a sin against his master, his mistress, himself and God.

When opportunities arise for us to benefit personally, financially, or professionally, do we consider the ramifications? What enables us to do the right thing? As a man of biblical faith, I have a concrete moral and ethical foundation on which I can lean when faced with any decision. Without this grounding, I'm afraid I might do whatever felt right in the moment. Isn't this the predicament of our society?

But once again, Joseph is at the mercy of those in power. His coat, in a *déjà vu* sort of way, is stripped from him as he flees Potiphar's wife. Who are people going to believe, the master's wife or the slave? So, he is thrown into prison where once again the Scriptures say, *"But the Lord was with Joseph."* Here he becomes the Warden's #1 man. Also, with God's help, he interprets the dreams of the imprisoned Cupbearer and Baker. Dreams which come true in a short amount of time.

But Joseph's imprisonment doesn't end quickly. The Cupbearer forgets the one who prophesied his release until Pharaoh himself has a dream. The Cupbearer remembers Joseph, and he is called to Pharaoh's court where, with God's help, he interprets the dream. And not only that, he casts a vision for its management, *"So let the king choose a man who is very wise and understanding and set him over the land of Egypt."* This could be an example of what we talked about in Career Prospectors where, I, as the job seeker, am seeking to solve the problems the employer has.

With this wisdom and advice, Joseph, probably much to the chagrin of Mrs. Potiphar, rose to be second only to Pharaoh in all of Egypt. One commentator noted, *"A good man will do good wherever he is, and will be a blessing even in bonds and banishment; for the Spirit of the Lord is never bound nor banished"* [Matthew Henry].

Application:
1) Our lives are not our own. What we do impacts everyone around us.
2) When we go through hardship, do we blame, try to learn, or simply accept things?
3) I've always understood the definition of integrity as, "Who are we when no one is looking?" How are you doing?
4) God's timing often involves suffering. What do you need to do to prepare yourself for difficult times?
5) Honor God above all else. A biblical foundation will provide resources unparalleled in our world.

*   *   *

*Respect for the Lord will teach you wisdom. If you want to be honored, you must be humble.*

(Proverbs 15:33)

# Day 13

We Begin with God's Word

Excerpts from Genesis 42-45

*When Jacob learned that there was grain in Egypt, he said to his sons, "Why do you just keep looking at each other?" He continued, "I have heard that there is grain in Egypt. Go down there and buy some for us, so that we may live and not die." Then ten of Joseph's brothers went down to buy grain from Egypt. But Jacob did not send Benjamin, Joseph's brother, with the others, because he was afraid that harm might come to him. So Israel's sons were among those who went to buy grain, for there was famine in the land of Canaan also.*

*Now Joseph was the governor of the land, the person who sold grain to all its people. So when Joseph's brothers arrived, they bowed down to him with their faces to the ground. As soon as Joseph saw his brothers, he recognized them, but he pretended to be a stranger and spoke harshly to them. "Where do you come from?" he asked. "From the land of Canaan," they replied, "to buy food." Although Joseph recognized his brothers, they did not recognize him. Then he remembered his dreams about them....*

*Then Joseph could no longer control himself before all his attendants, and he cried out, "Have everyone leave my presence!" So there was no one with Joseph when he made himself known to his brothers. And he wept so loudly that the Egyptians heard him, and Pharaoh's household heard about it.*

*Joseph said to his brothers, "I am Joseph! Is my father still living?" But his brothers were not able to answer him, because they were terrified at his presence. Then Joseph said to his brothers, "Come close to me." When they had done so, he said, "I am your brother Joseph, the one you sold into Egypt! And now, do not be distressed and do not be angry with yourselves for selling me here, because it was to save lives that God sent me ahead of you.*

# Joseph Part 3: Family Reunion

If I were to write Joseph's resume, I think it would look something like this:

The Resume of:
**Joseph**
(A Hebrew name meaning: "he will add")
*The son of Jacob*
aka
**Zaphenath-paneah**
(An Egyptian name meaning "the revealer of secrets or the god speaks and he lives")
*2nd only to Pharaoh*

Interpreter of Dreams    Righteous    Administrator

<u>Objective</u>: Submit to the will of God wherever I find myself

<u>Career Experience</u>:
**House Manager**        The Potiphar Household
1649-1647 BC
- *In charge of everything Potiphar owned and was not concerned about anything except the food he ate.* (Genesis 39:6)

**Warden's Assistant**    The Egyptian Prison System
1647-1645 BC
- *The warden paid no attention to anything that was in Joseph's care because the Lord was with Joseph and made him successful in everything he did.* (Genesis 39:23)

**Pharaoh's Chief of Staff**   All of Egypt
1645-1605 BC

- *No one in all the land of Egypt may lift a hand or a foot without my permission.*
  (Genesis 41:44)

If we look at Joseph's resume we might imagine that he never had any trouble. It does not state that he was disowned, became a slave, and was falsely accused and imprisoned for years. From 1649 to 1605 it appears like his career didn't have any hiccups or bumps in the road. Isn't this what we want on our resume? We do our best to cover up the ugly instances of getting fired or gaps in employment. But in actuality, by knowing Joseph's whole story we can really appreciate his character and understand his rise to fame.

From reading Genesis 42-45 we are not surprised that the other sons of Jacob never imagined that their brother Joseph, whom they sold into slavery, would rise to such a high position. How would that be possible? It's even less plausible than the executive who began in the mail room and rose to become the CEO. It's so impossible that when face to face with their brother, they do not recognize him.

But Joseph immediately recognizes them and in his shock puts them through a series of tests. He asks about their family and learns that his father is still alive. He puts the silver, with which they had purchased grain, back in their sacks. All seemingly to make sure that he gets to see them again.

The reunion finally comes when Joseph can't hold it in any longer, *"Joseph cried so loudly that the Egyptians heard him, and the people in the king's palace heard about it. He said to his brothers, "I am Joseph. Is my father still alive?" But the brothers could not answer him, because they were very afraid of him."* Yeah.....terrified, bewildered, stunned. The writer makes it clear that his brothers figured that Joseph, very naturally, would now get his revenge.

Instead, Joseph, imagining what they're thinking says, *"Now don't be worried or angry with yourselves because you sold me here. God sent me here ahead of you to save people's lives."* What incredible forgiveness and insight! Not only did he rise to power from slavery but he also grew in character. He matured beyond his brothers as God used him to not only save a nation but to fulfill a prophecy that God gave to Abraham many years before: *"You can be sure that your descendants will be strangers and travel in a land they don't own. The people there will make them slaves and be cruel to them for four hundred years"* (Genesis 15:13). But that's another story.

Application:
1. When writing a resume, certainly emphasize the high points, but be ready to tell the in-between stories too.
2. Make the best of difficult circumstances by trusting in the sovereignty of God.
3. Remember to 'grow where you are planted' rather than pine away for that elusive position that may or may not come.
4. If you have ever been in the position of Joseph's brothers remember that God can even use our mistakes. But learn from those mistakes.
5. Forgiveness is more powerful than revenge.

\*   \*   \*

*But Joseph said to them, "Don't be afraid. Am I in the place of God? You intended to harm me, but God intended it for good to accomplish what is now being done, the saving of many lives.*

(Genesis 50:19,20)

# Day 14

We Begin with God's Word

Excerpts from Exodus 35

*Moses assembled the whole Israelite community and said to them, "These are the things the Lord has commanded you to do: For six days, work is to be done, but the seventh day shall be your holy day, a day of sabbath rest to the Lord. Whoever does any work on it is to be put to death. Do not light a fire in any of your dwellings on the Sabbath day..."*

*Then the whole Israelite community withdrew from Moses' presence, and everyone who was willing and whose heart moved them came and brought an offering to the Lord for the work on the tent of meeting, for all its service, and for the sacred garments. ....*

*Every skilled woman spun with her hands and brought what she had spun—blue, purple or scarlet yarn or fine linen. And all the women who were willing and had the skill spun the goat hair. The leaders brought onyx stones and other gems to be mounted on the ephod and breastpiece. They also brought spices and olive oil for the light and for the anointing oil and for the fragrant incense. All the Israelite men and women who were willing brought to the Lord freewill offerings for all the work the Lord through Moses had commanded them to do.*

*Then Moses said to the Israelites, "See, the Lord has chosen Bezalel son of Uri, the son of Hur, of the tribe of Judah, and he has filled him with the Spirit of God, with wisdom, with understanding, with knowledge and with all kinds of skills— to make artistic designs for work in gold, silver and bronze, to cut and set stones, to work in wood and to engage in all kinds of artistic crafts. And he has given both him and Oholiab son of Ahisamak, of the tribe of Dan, the ability to teach others. He has filled them with skill to do all kinds of work as engravers, designers, embroiderers in blue, purple and scarlet yarn and fine linen, and weavers—all of them skilled workers and designers.*

# Avodah
# Work and Worship

We are very familiar with the word work. We go to work. We work out in the yard. We have to do work in order to earn a paycheck. Work is often viewed as a necessary evil. Thus, the extreme, concentrated effort toward preparing for retirement, that time when we don't have to work any more. We are less accustomed to the word worship. If we were to do a word association game I wonder what you would come up with. My guess is "church", "hymn singing," "hands raised," "angels," you might remember people in the Bible falling on their faces before angels, fire on the mountain and even the people in the New Testament who recognized Jesus as God.

Can you imagine any two words that seem so different? Yet they have their origins in the same Hebrew word, a*vodah*. We are so far removed from Hebrew culture that the idea that these words could be integrally related is hard to imagine. We are more likely to relate to the Greek culture, a little more closely connected in time and space with regards to our Western mindset; a worldview that says work is secular and worship is sacred. What if the two were more closely aligned in our minds? Would this cause confusion or would it provide more certainty in discovering our purpose?

A lot of personality tests distinguish between two polar opposites: the task-oriented person and the people-oriented person. I'm the task type. I like lists. I like to check boxes. I like to start a job, have a deadline and finish on time. Ironic that God called me into the ministry where I work primarily with people.

Throughout my career I have had to be entirely dependent upon God to help me be effective and not view people as projects. I recognize my weakness in this area but it seems that God likes it this way.

As a task-oriented person, I have never connected work and worship. Even though I have been a paid religious professional, my distortion and misunderstanding of the interrelatedness of work and worship has hindered my effectiveness in living out my call and from convincingly preaching that the two are one. A friend and I looked at Exodus 35 the other day and noted how the work that they were commanded to do directly related to the worship of God:

- Clear distinction between six days of work and one day of Sabbath. Not that one was secular and the other sacred but all was to be done for the glory of God and for our good.
- Our skills and talents are given by God and we are to use them for his glory.
- Our charitable giving is a response to God's goodness.

This combats the notion that religious work is more "holy" than secular work. If we see Scripture with the lens that work and worship are interrelated then we will clearly see that nothing is wholly sacred or wholly secular, all is holy. The biblical worldview is that all that is good comes from God. Exodus 35 teaches that our creativity and ingenuity are what make us human. When used to the glory of God the most mundane of all tasks can be seen with ultimate purpose. A job, a career, an occupation, whatever you want to call it, is not just something we do until we can retire, but it's the human way of being our true selves six days a week.

Then on the seventh we rest. But all seven days we worship through our work.

One of my heroes is a man named Dois Rosser, founder of International Cooperating Ministries. Up until age 65 he built a financial kingdom through car dealerships and smart investments. Upon 'retirement' he knew that God was calling him to do something that would connect his work and worship. He teamed up with his pastor and together that created a ministry that has built more than 9,000 churches around the world. He recently passed from this world and bucked the trend that working life ends at 65 by continuing to do what became his lifework for another 33 years.

Imagine what we can do if we will adopt the worldview that our a*vodah* is one. What will we find ourselves doing by discovering our true purpose?

Application:
1. What can you do if you consider your work a grind? What would it look like to do everything as unto the Lord?
2. Are you more task-oriented or people-oriented? What are the advantages and disadvantages of each?
3. What benefits are there to practicing a regular Sabbath?
4. What's your view of retirement? What if, like Dois Rosser, you discovered your lifework in your fifties and sixties?
5. We hear a lot of talk about doing what you love. If we understand a*vodah* wouldn't it be possible to love whatever we find ourselves doing rather than reaching for something for which we are ill-equipped?

*　　*　　*

*He has filled them with skill to do all kinds of work as engravers, designers, embroiderers in blue, purple and scarlet yarn and fine linen, and weavers—all of them skilled workers and designers.*

(Exodus 35:35)

# Day 15

We Begin with God's Word

Excerpts from Exodus 3 & 4

*…The Lord said, "I have indeed seen the misery of my people in Egypt. I have heard them crying out because of their slave drivers, and I am concerned about their suffering. So I have come down to rescue them from the hand of the Egyptians and to bring them up out of that land into a good and spacious land, a land flowing with milk and honey…So now, go. I am sending you to Pharaoh to bring my people the Israelites out of Egypt." But Moses said to God, "Who am I that I should go to Pharaoh and bring the Israelites out of Egypt?" And God said, "I will be with you…"*

*Moses said to God, "Suppose I go to the Israelites and say to them, 'The God of your fathers has sent me to you,' and they ask me, 'What is his name?' Then what shall I tell them?" God said to Moses, "I am who I am…"*

*"The elders of Israel will listen to you. Then you and the elders are to go to the king of Egypt and say to him, 'The Lord, the God of the Hebrews, has met with us. Let us take a three-day journey into the wilderness to offer sacrifices to the Lord our God.' But I know that the king of Egypt will not let you go unless a mighty hand compels him. So I will stretch out my hand and strike the Egyptians with all the wonders that I will perform among them. After that, he will let you go…"*

*Then the Lord said to him, "What is that in your hand?" "A staff," he replied. The Lord said, "Throw it on the ground." Moses threw it on the ground and it became a snake, and he ran from it. Then the Lord said to him, "Reach out your hand and take it by the tail." So Moses reached out and took hold of the snake and it turned back into a staff in his hand. Then the Lord said, "Put your hand inside your cloak." So Moses put his hand into his cloak, and when he took it out, the skin was leprous—it had become as white as snow. "Now put it back into your cloak," he said. So Moses put his hand back into his cloak, and when he took it out, it was restored, like the rest of his flesh…"*

*Moses said to the Lord, "Pardon your servant, Lord. I have never been eloquent, neither in the past nor since you have spoken to your servant. I am slow of speech and tongue." The Lord said to him, "Who gave human beings their mouths? Who makes them deaf or mute? Is it not I, the Lord? Now go; I will help you speak and will teach you what to say." But Moses said, "Pardon your servant, Lord. Please send someone else."*

*Then the Lord's anger burned against Moses and he said, "What about your brother, Aaron the Levite? I know he can speak well. He is already on his way to meet you, and he will be glad to see you. You shall speak to him and put words in his mouth; I will help both of you speak and will teach you what to do. He will speak to the people for you, and it will be as if he were your mouth and as if you were God to him. But take this staff in your hand so you can perform the signs with it…"*

## Moses' Objections...and Ours

Moses is now in his second career. His first being a prince of Egypt for about 40 years. His second...a shepherd in the desert working for his father-in-law for another 40 years. Now God is calling him to his third... God's spokesman or Israel's deliverer. Moses had been born to Amram and Jochebed, Hebrew slaves, but he was raised in Pharaoh's palace as a prince of Egypt.

How long had Moses known that he was a Hebrew? Maybe he thought he might be the next Joseph and he was biding his time while he figured out a plan to rescue his people. Pharaoh must have known Moses' heredity, and yet he still raised him as a son. All is going fine until Moses "exercises his leadership skills" and kills an Egyptian for abusing a Hebrew slave. He thinks this crime has gone unnoticed until he gets into the middle of a fight between two Israelites, and they reveal that news of his reputation as a murderer had indeed spread.

Escaping to the desert, you may picture the handsome Charlton Heston rescuing Jethro's daughters in Cecil B. Demille's "Ten Commandments". It's there that he seemingly settles into a whole new life. Until the burning bush incident. Many of us have had experiences where we sensed a change of career was coming, even called it our 'burning bush moment'. It would mean a 180° switch. We might even say, 'this new job or career is what I'm made for.' But, like Moses, some of us may have been reluctant to change.

Let's examine five objections that Moses had and discover if we see ourselves in them.

Application:

**Objection #1:** "Who am I that I should go to Pharaoh and bring the Israelites out of Egypt?"

Understandably, Moses had 40 years to get used to the idea of being a shepherd. All his princely training was out the window. At the age of 80 or so, he was probably quite content to spend his last days with the sheep in the wilderness. But God had a different idea.

**God's answer:** *"I will be with you. And this will be the sign to you that it is I who have sent you: When you have brought the people out of Egypt, you will worship God on this mountain."*

Why would Moses say "No" to that? God's presence today is no less real, and yet we often experience our jobs, conflicts, and unemployment as if we have to cope with them all alone. Let God's promise resonate in you... *"I will be with you"*.

**Objection #2:** *"Suppose I go to the Israelites and say to them, 'The God of your fathers has sent me to you,' and they ask me, 'What is his name?' Then what shall I tell them?"*

Great question? Moses was probably just a legend at this point, unheard of for 40 years, and now he's supposed to go back with a message from God? When I went home one night a few years ago and suggested that we move overseas and that God told me to, can you imagine my wife's response?

**God's answer:** *"I am who I am."*

I can hear Moses thinking, okay, Lord, can you be more specific?! This is not what he is expecting. The

Hebrew spelling looks something like *Yahweh*, and it means "God is." God is not past, present, or future. He is outside of time. He is omnipotent, omniscient, and omnipresent (all-powerful, all-knowing, and everywhere always). Does this sound like a God who can do something about your current difficult situation, whether it be an illness, unemployment, or conflict?

**Objection #3:** *"What if they do not believe me or listen to me and say, 'The Lord did not appear to you'?"*

I think that's reasonable. They could respond to Moses with, "Your name again is ___? You say you grew up here? You've been in the desert so long your brains are fried. You expect us to believe that THE God appeared to just you, and not all of us?! I don't think so." But God did speak to Moses, and he still speaks today, through his Word and his Holy Spirit. In practical ways which speak to us in every avenue of life, God speaks to us, even in regards to our careers.

**God's answer:** Check this out. *"Throw your staff on the ground."* It becomes a snake. *"Stick your hand in your cloak."* It becomes leprous. *"Put it back in."* It is restored. *"Throw this water in the Nile".* It turns to blood."

With these miracles, God helped Moses convince the people that he was no ordinary guy. Honestly, I'd like to see confirmation like that in my life. Imagine having a choice between two good things and this big arrow comes from heaven and points me in the right direction. But I suppose God doesn't work like that anymore. We do have the Bible though. Something Moses didn't have yet.

**Objection #4:** *"Pardon your servant, Lord. I have never been eloquent, neither in the past nor since you have spoken to your servant. I am slow of speech and tongue."*

Do I detect whining here? And whining is not reserved for eight year olds who don't get their way. I've heard many adults carry on some serious whining when they felt left out, unheard or looked over. Why do you think the Apostle Paul commands us to *"Do everything without complaining?"* Because we do it so well.

**God's Answer:** *"Who gave human beings their mouths? Who makes them deaf or mute? Who gives them sight or makes them blind? Is it not I, the Lord? Now go; I will help you speak and will teach you what to say."*

Another good answer. Is it becoming clear that it's hard to argue with God? Can this be applied also to the jobs to which he has called us? We may find ourselves in over our heads but that's when faith becomes real. God loves it when we have to depend upon Him. It's then that He gets the credit for the seemingly impossible. Do you feel like you are in an impossible situation?

**Objection #5:** *"Pardon your servant, Lord. Please send someone else."*

Since God had an answer for every one of his objections, this seems like the only way out. It reminds me of friends who are recently unemployed and for a couple of weeks just lie around the house feeling worthless. Receiving a 'pink slip' can suck the life out of any motivation we might have to move forward. Naturally, we collapse in a corner and have our little pity party. This is what happens when we think we're all alone. But God has an answer even for this objection.

**God's answer:** *Then the Lord's anger burned against Moses and he said, "What about your brother, Aaron the Levite? I know he can speak well. He is already on his way to meet you, and he will be glad to see you. You shall speak to him and put words in his mouth; I will help both of you speak and will teach you what to do."*

Moses has ticked God off. Of course, God could have chosen someone else. Sometimes, on any given day, I wonder if God has chosen me for the particular predicament in which I find myself. (Someone has even said, *"God has entrusted you with this problem."*) We seem to grow better when faced with difficulty. Again, the Apostle Paul tells us that *"suffering produces perseverance; perseverance, character; and character, hope. And hope does not put us to shame, because God's love has been poured out into our hearts through the Holy Spirit, who has been given to us"* (Romans 5:3-5).

So, what's your question or objection for God? He will not be surprised and He will answer you. Actually, He's given us the answer even before the question is formed on our lips. And the best way we can know it is through reading the Bible. Everything we need to know is at our finger tips. The sad truth is that for many of us, the Bible sits on our shelf unopened. I pray that you would know the hope that is available to you today. Open it.

\* \* \*

*I pray that the eyes of your heart may be enlightened in order that you may know the hope to which he has called you, the riches of his glorious inheritance in his holy people, and his incomparably great power for us who believe.*

(Ephesians 1:18-19)

# Day 16

We Begin with God's Word

Exodus 17:8-14

*The Amalekites came and attacked the Israelites at Rephidim. Moses said to Joshua, "Choose some of our men and go out to fight the Amalekites. Tomorrow I will stand on top of the hill with the staff of God in my hands." So Joshua fought the Amalekites as Moses had ordered, and Moses, Aaron and Hur went to the top of the hill. As long as Moses held up his hands, the Israelites were winning, but whenever he lowered his hands, the Amalekites were winning. When Moses' hands grew tired, they took a stone and put it under him and he sat on it. Aaron and Hur held his hands up—one on one side, one on the other—so that his hands remained steady till sunset. So Joshua overcame the Amalekite army with the sword. Then the Lord said to Moses, "Write this on a scroll as something to be remembered and make sure that Joshua hears it, because I will completely blot out the name of Amalek from under heaven."*

Exodus 24:13-18

*Then Moses set out with Joshua his aide, and Moses went up on the mountain of God. He said to the elders, "Wait here for us until we come back to you. Aaron and Hur are with you, and anyone involved in a dispute can go to them." When Moses went up on the mountain, the cloud covered it, and the glory of the Lord settled on Mount Sinai. For six days the cloud covered the mountain, and on the seventh day the Lord called to Moses from within the cloud. To the Israelites the glory of the Lord looked like a consuming fire on top of the mountain. Then Moses entered the cloud as he went on up the mountain. And he stayed on the mountain forty days and forty nights.*

Numbers 14:6-12

*Joshua son of Nun and Caleb son of Jephunneh, who were among those who had explored the land, tore their clothes and said to the entire Israelite assembly, "The land we passed through and explored is exceedingly good. If the Lord is pleased with us, he will lead us into that land, a land flowing with milk and honey, and will give it to us. Only do not rebel against the Lord. And do not be afraid of the people of the land, because we will devour them. Their protection is gone, but the Lord is with us. Do not be afraid of them." But the whole assembly talked about stoning them. Then the glory of the Lord appeared at the tent of meeting to all the Israelites. The Lord said to Moses, "How long will these people treat me with contempt? How long will they refuse to believe in me, in spite of all the signs I have performed among them? I will strike them down with a plague and destroy them, but I will make you into a nation greater and stronger than they."*

## Joshua: Military Leader and Aide to Moses

I enjoyed reading the autobiography of Colin Powell, who was born in 1937 to parents of Jamaican descent, grew to adulthood during a tumultuous time of racism, and exceeded many expectations of what a black man could accomplish in America. The part of his life that amazed me was that as a four-star general he was willing to enter the political world and serve as senior military assistant to the Secretary of Defense. He said he would rather be in the military, where he felt his gifts and skills would most logically be used, but he was willing to submit to those in authority over him.

We discover Joshua in the pages of Exodus and like Colin Powell, he makes his debut as a military leader. Under the authority of Moses, he defeated the enemies of Israel as they crossed the desert. In the very first battle it's clear that God's sovereignty was in play as he commanded Moses to stand on a hill with his staff raised over his head while Joshua went into battle against the Amalekites. Whenever the staff was raised God gave Joshua victory. If Moses' arms got tired, the Israelites were beaten back. In the end, Moses, Joshua and the Israelites were victorious.

Moses did not praise Joshua for the victory, but set up an altar to God in honor of this battle, where it was evident that God's favor was upon Israel. A pattern that when practiced, gave Israel the security that God would fulfill his vow to bring them into the promised land. Joshua's military career takes a turn as Moses chooses him as his personal aide. Is this a promotion? A proper use of Joshua's skills? Moses may have been thinking that he would not always be around and that he would need a successor and this young man fit the bill.

As his aide, Joshua stayed close to Moses' side. When Moses went up the mountain to receive the Law from God, Joshua went with him. For forty days and nights, Joshua was either with Moses or very close to the conversation between him and God. Another time when it was clear that Joshua had a privileged position was when Moses set up a tent where the presence of God appeared as a cloud descending upon it. Moses would leave the tent and Joshua would remain. We can only imagine what this experience was like for him.

The defining episode in Joshua's life occurred when he and the other eleven representatives from the twelve tribes of Israel went to explore the promised land. Ten came back fearful, proclaiming *"The land we explored devours those living in it."* But Caleb, of the tribe of Judah (ancestor of Jesus) and Joshua of the tribe of Ephraim argued, *"We should go up and take possession of the land, for we can certainly do it."* This rebellion condemned the Israelites to wander in the desert for forty years. Everyone over the age of twenty perished in the wilderness.

The people of Israel were led astray by those who had not remembered God's miraculous hand upon them. Caleb and Joshua stood apart from them, as godly men who trusted in God's promises despite appearances to the contrary. The question today is, "Will I be a Caleb or a Joshua willing to be the man or woman willing to do the right thing regardless of the obstacles?" What circumstances am I in that are challenging my character and my faith?

Application:
1. What are my gifts and skills? Am I using them to the best of my ability and to the glory of God? In what ways?

2. If chosen for a task that I wouldn't necessarily choose for myself, how will I know if God wants me to say "Yes" or "No"?
3. When I have accomplished great things, how do I receive praise? How can I give glory to God?
4. Have I had times in my life when it was clear that God spoke to me? Did this influence my character development? Did I change? Today, regardless of my current circumstances do I know who I am according to God's Word?
5. If everyone spoke against what I knew to be the clear will of God am I willing to stand my ground regardless of the consequences?

\*  \*  \*

*But if serving the Lord seems undesirable to you, then choose for yourselves this day whom you will serve, whether the gods your ancestors served beyond the Euphrates, or the gods of the Amorites, in whose land you are living. But as for me and my household, we will serve the Lord.*
(Joshua 24:15)

# Day 17

We Begin with God's Word

Joshua 24:1-26

*Then Joshua assembled all the tribes of Israel at Shechem. He summoned the elders, leaders, judges and officials of Israel, and they presented themselves before God. Joshua said to all the people, "This is what the Lord, the God of Israel, says: 'Long ago your ancestors, including Terah the father of Abraham and Nahor, lived beyond the Euphrates River and worshiped other gods. But I took your father Abraham from the land beyond the Euphrates and led him throughout Canaan and gave him many descendants. I gave him Isaac, and to Isaac I gave Jacob and Esau. I assigned the hill country of Seir to Esau, but Jacob and his family went down to Egypt.*

*"'Then I sent Moses and Aaron, and I afflicted the Egyptians by what I did there, and I brought you out. When I brought your people out of Egypt, you came to the sea, and the Egyptians pursued them with chariots and horsemen as far as the Red Sea. But they cried to the Lord for help, and he put darkness between you and the Egyptians; he brought the sea over them and covered them. You saw with your own eyes what I did to the Egyptians. Then you lived in the wilderness for a long time.*

*"'I brought you to the land of the Amorites who lived east of the Jordan. They fought against you, but I gave them into your hands. I destroyed them from before you, and you took possession of their land. When Balak son of Zippor, the king of Moab, prepared to fight*

*against Israel, he sent for Balaam son of Beor to put a curse on you. But I would not listen to Balaam, so he blessed you again and again, and I delivered you out of his hand. "'Then you crossed the Jordan and came to Jericho. The citizens of Jericho fought against you, as did also the Amorites, Perizzites, Canaanites, Hittites, Girgashites, Hivites and Jebusites, but I gave them into your hands. I sent the hornet ahead of you, which drove them out before you—also the two Amorite kings. You did not do it with your own sword and bow. So I gave you a land on which you did not toil and cities you did not build; and you live in them and eat from vineyards and olive groves that you did not plant.'*

"Now fear the Lord and serve him with all faithfulness. Throw away the gods your ancestors worshiped beyond the Euphrates River and in Egypt, and serve the Lord. But if serving the Lord seems undesirable to you, then choose for yourselves this day whom you will serve, whether the gods your ancestors served beyond the Euphrates, or the gods of the Amorites, in whose land you are living. But as for me and my household, we will serve the Lord."

Then the people answered, "Far be it from us to forsake the Lord to serve other gods! It was the Lord our God himself who brought us and our parents up out of Egypt, from that land of slavery, and performed those great signs before our eyes. He protected us on our entire journey and among all the nations through which we traveled. And the Lord drove out before us all the nations, including the Amorites, who lived in the land. We too will serve the Lord, because he is our God."

*Joshua said to the people, "You are not able to serve the Lord. He is a holy God; he is a jealous God. He will not forgive your rebellion and your sins. If you forsake the Lord and serve foreign gods, he will turn and bring disaster on you and make an end of you, after he has been good to you." But the people said to Joshua, "No! We will serve the Lord." Then Joshua said, "You are witnesses against yourselves that you have chosen to serve the Lord."*

*"Yes, we are witnesses," they replied. "Now then," said Joshua, "throw away the foreign gods that are among you and yield your hearts to the Lord, the God of Israel." And the people said to Joshua, "We will serve the Lord our God and obey him."*

*On that day Joshua made a covenant for the people, and there at Shechem he reaffirmed for them decrees and laws. And Joshua recorded these things in the Book of the Law of God. Then he took a large stone and set it up there under the oak near the holy place of the Lord.*

# Joshua: Leader of Israel

Are leaders born? Are they made? I remember my sixth grade teacher asking who we thought were leaders in our class. At the mention of my name, a brash young man laughed at the idea that I might be a leader. At eleven years old why did I care? I should not have been surprised or hurt, but I was. But why? What qualities did I desire or did I think a leader possessed? As we transition from the book of Exodus to Joshua, two young men stand out above all the others: Caleb and Joshua. And yet it's Joshua who rises to become the successor of Moses.

Did Joshua have gifts and skills that Caleb didn't or was he simply chosen by God? Sometimes in our jobs it seems like it's just a matter of being in the right place at the right time. Others may get promoted over us and we have a choice as to how to react. I wish we knew more about Caleb, but I'll give him the benefit of the doubt that he gladly served Joshua because he could see God's hand was upon him.

Joshua had successfully served as Israel's military leader and Moses' aide. He had been privy to conversations between God and Moses on the mountain and in the tent when God's presence came in a cloud. We read in Deuteronomy 34:9, *"Now Joshua son of Nun was filled with the spirit of wisdom because Moses had laid his hands on him."*

In the interplay between the gifts that God gives us and how we handle those gifts, I believe that there has to be a sense of cooperation between God's sovereign choice and our actions. Too many great men of God have fallen, to dispute this. Pastors and leaders who I have admired, and who were obviously gifted by God in skill and wisdom chose to succumb to the baser qualities of human nature. The beauty of the gospel is that we can be restored to communion with God, but the consequences of our actions will not be erased.

Of course, Joshua was human and at least one time he forgot to inquire of the Lord when the Gibeonites deceived him. But in most cases Joshua honored God throughout the conquest of the Promised Land. It wasn't easy. Several times, it's repeated, *"Be strong and courageous."* Why be strong and courageous? Because enemies, deception, and fear were forcing the people of Israel to fully depend upon God.

In the midst of having victory after victory, one man still chose a life of deception. Achan disobeyed the Lord's command by keeping some of the riches from one of their battles. Joshua had to pass judgment, according to God's Law, so Achan was stoned to death. We can't fully understand the implications and the historical context, but the point is that God's holiness had been compromised, and a severe penalty was required. The best thing that can be said of Joshua was that, *"As the Lord commanded his servant Moses, so Moses commanded Joshua, and Joshua did it; he left nothing undone of all that the Lord commanded Moses."*

In Joshua's farewell speech he reminds the people of their history. For the past 40 years God has not failed you. You must continue to be strong and courageous. Every day you must choose whom you will serve. You can't do it yourselves. Remember the consequences of disobedience.

His speech in Joshua 24 is harsh. He knows all too well the tendencies of his people. He demonstrates the need of daily dependence upon God for strength to resist the temptation to fall into the practices of the cultures around them. God's sovereignty could certainly have protected them, but the way it seems that God works, he wants us to demonstrate our love for him through obedience. His unconditional love is always there, but to experience his ongoing conditional love or blessing there must be a regular practice of submission, confession, repentance and worship.

Application:
1. Are you a leader? Where do your principles come from?
2. Has someone been recognized or promoted instead of you? How can you be like Caleb and serve them seeking their good and the good of the business?
3. When you make mistakes do you readily confess and repent? What remains unfinished in your life in this regard?
4. I believe it does matter what people think of you, because our values and commitments represent One greater than us. How can you be strong and courageous today demonstrating faith in God and the desire to serve him wholeheartedly?

\*　　\*　　\*

*"A good name is more desirable than great riches; to be esteemed is better than silver or gold."*
(Proverbs 22:1)

# Day 18

We Begin with God's Word

An Excerpt from Judges 4

*Again the Israelites did evil in the eyes of the Lord, now that Ehud was dead. So the Lord sold them into the hands of Jabin king of Canaan, who reigned in Hazor. Sisera, the commander of his army, was based in Harosheth Haggoyim. Because he had nine hundred chariots fitted with iron and had cruelly oppressed the Israelites for twenty years, they cried to the Lord for help.*

*Now Deborah, a prophet, the wife of Lappidoth, was leading Israel at that time. She held court under the Palm of Deborah between Ramah and Bethel in the hill country of Ephraim, and the Israelites went up to her to have their disputes decided. She sent for Barak son of Abinoam from Kedesh in Naphtali and said to him, "The Lord, the God of Israel, commands you: 'Go, take with you ten thousand men of Naphtali and Zebulun and lead them up to Mount Tabor. I will lead Sisera, the commander of Jabin's army, with his chariots and his troops to the Kishon River and give him into your hands.'" Barak said to her, "If you go with me, I will go; but if you don't go with me, I won't go." "Certainly I will go with you," said Deborah. "But because of the course you are taking, the honor will not be yours, for the Lord will deliver Sisera into the hands of a woman…"*

*Then Deborah said to Barak, "Go! This is the day the Lord has given Sisera into your hands. Has not the Lord gone ahead of you?" So Barak went down Mount Tabor, with ten thousand men following him. At*

*Barak's advance, the Lord routed Sisera and all his chariots and army by the sword, and Sisera got down from his chariot and fled on foot...*

*Jael went out to meet Sisera and said to him, "Come, my lord, come right in. Don't be afraid." So he entered her tent, and she covered him with a blanket. "I'm thirsty," he said. "Please give me some water." She opened a skin of milk, gave him a drink, and covered him up. "Stand in the doorway of the tent," he told her. "If someone comes by and asks you, 'Is anyone in there?' say 'No.'" But Jael, Heber's wife, picked up a tent peg and a hammer and went quietly to him while he lay fast asleep, exhausted. She drove the peg through his temple into the ground, and he died...*

# Deborah: Prophetess, Judge and Team-player

Many of us love to watch sports, not just for the great win, but to watch the teamwork and observe the attitudes of such talented men and women. But many a career has been sacrificed to the idol of arrogance. Two athletes come to mind; who could've been great, but their narcissism cut short their careers.

As talented as Bill Romanowski was during his career, it would not be a stretch to suggest that the NFL would have been better off had he and others like him never played in the league. Romanowski was involved in multiple unflattering incidents as a player, the worst of which probably being when he clocked teammate Marcus Williams. That incident left Williams with serious injuries that ended his career.

Randy Moss may be the most talented wide receiver in the history of the NFL (even better than Jerry Rice). Moss showed that he was a once-in-a-generation talent during his best seasons with Tom Brady and the New England Patriots. The shame of Moss' career is that he eventually wore out his welcome with every team that gave him a shot. Teams need cooperation and collaboration more than they need superstars.

The question we have to ask is: "What about me?" Am I a good team player? Do our co-workers request our participation or our resignation? As we look at the ancient book of Judges in the Old Testament of the Bible we find many examples of good and bad team players. Deborah, the prophetess, is an example of someone who found herself in a role of leadership because God's hand was upon her. The general who led the military of Israel, Barak, was a fighting man, but he recognized his limitations as a leader and employed Deborah as his partner to defeat Israel's enemies.

The story begins with Israel's faithless behavior. A repeated refrain, *"Again Israel did evil in the eyes of the Lord"* leads off our passage. Obedience would have simplified their lives but God does not leave them without hope. (He even told Moses dozens of years earlier, *"when you and your children return to the Lord your God and obey him with all your heart and with all your soul according to everything I command you today, then the Lord your God will restore your fortunes and have compassion on you and gather you again from all the nations where he scattered you."*) For eighty years Israel had enjoyed prosperity because of God's blessings, but their success led them to forget their devotion to God. They grew fat and lazy and worshiped foreign gods rather than the one true God.

In this period of time, a judge arose to govern God's people. Deborah, a woman to whom God spoke, called Barak and issued God's command to fight against his enemy Sisera. Barak was willing to obey with the condition that Deborah go with him as his military advisor. He had no doubt of his military strength, but he also recognized that Deborah had an "in" with God.

For Deborah, the command of God was enough. God would fight for Israel. But for Barak, he needed some reassurance and, contrary to the custom of the day, he showed great humility toward Deborah in asking her to accompany him. Even if it meant losing recognition in the eyes of the people, Barak didn't seem to care. He knew he could lead men into battle, but he also knew that without God, victory would be denied. The battle ended swiftly, *"Barak pursued the chariots and army as far as Harosheth Haggoyim, and all Sisera's troops fell by the sword; not a man was left."*

A commentator said, *"He could do nothing without her head, nor she without his hands; but both together made a complete deliverer, and effected a complete deliverance. The greatest and best are not self-sufficient, but need one another."* [Matthew Henry]

Application:
1) Israel had forgotten their calling as God's chosen people. Deborah stood apart in her devotion to God. When have you taken a moral stand against the prevailing immoral climate?
2) When have you experienced the consequences of success, grown soft, arrogant, or naive?
3) Will we be like Barak, willing to receive advice and guidance from a 'Deborah' who may not have the same experience or expertise?
4) If someone was more qualified for a job, would you be willing to suggest them over yourself? What are the benefits or consequences of such an act?
5) Our influence, character, and wisdom go beyond our practical knowledge. Have you been asked to be part of something you knew little about, simply because your friend/boss valued your opinion? What was the result?

\*    \*    \*

*The fear of the Lord is the beginning of knowledge, but fools despise wisdom and instruction.*
(Proverbs 1:7)

# Day 19

We Begin with God's Word

Matthew 2:1-18

*After Jesus was born in Bethlehem in Judea, during the time of King Herod, Magi from the east came to Jerusalem and asked, "Where is the one who has been born king of the Jews? We saw his star when it rose and have come to worship him." When King Herod heard this he was disturbed, and all Jerusalem with him. When he had called together all the people's chief priests and teachers of the law, he asked them where the Messiah was to be born. "In Bethlehem in Judea," they replied, "for this is what the prophet has written:*

*"'But you, Bethlehem, in the land of Judah,*
*are by no means least among the rulers of Judah;*
*for out of you will come a ruler*
*who will shepherd my people Israel.'"*

*Then Herod called the Magi secretly and found out from them the exact time the star had appeared. He sent them to Bethlehem and said, "Go and search carefully for the child. As soon as you find him, report to me, so that I too may go and worship him." After they had heard the king, they went on their way, and the star they had seen when it rose went ahead of them until it stopped over the place where the child was. When they saw the star, they were overjoyed. On coming to the house, they saw the child with his mother Mary, and they bowed down and worshiped him. Then they opened their treasures and presented him with gifts of gold, frankincense and myrrh. And having been warned in a dream not to go back to Herod, they returned to their country by another route.*

*When they had gone, an angel of the Lord appeared to Joseph in a dream. "Get up," he said, "take the child and his mother and escape to Egypt. Stay there until I tell you, for Herod is going to search for the child to kill him." So he got up, took the child and his mother during the night and left for Egypt, where he stayed until the death of Herod. And so was fulfilled what the Lord had said through the prophet: "Out of Egypt I called my son."*

*When Herod realized that he had been outwitted by the Magi, he was furious, and he gave orders to kill all the boys in Bethlehem and its vicinity who were two years old and under, in accordance with the time he had learned from the Magi. Then what was said through the prophet Jeremiah was fulfilled:*

> *"A voice is heard in Ramah,*
> *weeping and great mourning,*
> *Rachel weeping for her children*
> *and refusing to be comforted,*
> *because they are no more."*

# Actions of the Wise
*What the Magi have to teach us*

What makes someone wise? Can we tell by what they say - or don't say? *"Even fools are thought wise if they keep silent, and discerning if they hold their tongues,"* says Proverbs 17:28.

Were the Magi, or Wise Men, of two thousand years ago, particularly "wise"? Or was that just another name or title for Eastern kings or Astrologers? What can we learn about them from today's passage that can inform how we face the workplace?

We don't know how many wise men there were: we have assumed there were three because they brought three gifts, but our passage does not declare a number. From historical records we know that they were men who studied the stars and tried to interpret the times according to the movement of the constellations. This star that appeared in the east surprised them and beckoned them to follow its tail to a place to which it was pointing.

Upon getting close to its source they came to the capital of the once great Jewish nation, Jerusalem. It made sense to inquire within about the star for surely they would have already been studying it. They seemed to present new information, however, for King Herod and all Jerusalem were disturbed by these foreigners who came from the east to seek the newborn king of the Jews. Proud men and fearful people do not like to be told something that they should already know.

Herod does his homework by asking the resident theologians about the birth of the Messiah. He discovers that it will occur in Bethlehem, the city of David, a small town about six miles away. He then concocts a lie, telling the wise men to bring him news of this new king, so that he too may go and worship him. Couldn't he have traveled there himself?

When the Magi do not report back, Herod, in a fit of rage, orders the execution of all baby boys two and younger. We should not be surprised considering that this is the same man who killed his own two sons so that they would not be a threat to his reign. One commentator states, *"We cannot expect too little from man, nor too much from God."* Later in his adult life Jesus demonstrates his own distrust in people who try to forcibly make him king. John 2:24,25 says, *"But Jesus would not entrust himself to them, for he knew all people. He did not need any testimony about mankind, for he knew what was in each person."*

Why doesn't God intervene? And why doesn't he miraculously protect His own son? For surely He could have called down an army of angels which were at His disposal. Years later Jesus tells Pilate, *"Do you think I cannot call on my Father, and he will at once put at my disposal more than twelve legions of angels?"* Instead God told Mary and Joseph to flee to Egypt.

We never hear anymore about the Wise Men in recorded biblical history. Was this an unprecedented event in their lives? I assume they discovered the uniqueness of the good news they heard proclaimed, that it replaced preconceived beliefs about deity, life's purpose, and supernatural intervention. How could they look at the stars the same way after that?

What does the Wise Men's obedience to the dream, and not to the king, tell us about handling deceitful people? Certainly, not giving them the benefit of the doubt. Herod's pride and the people's fear were some of the primary reasons Jesus came in the first place. If we surrender doubt and fear to God in worship, we will discover true freedom. The wise men were open to discovering the Truth, whereas, Herod demonstrated his commitment to self-preservation and deceit.

Application:
1. What can you do when your supervisor/employer lies or asks you to be deceitful?
2. When have you done the right thing with right motives, but it seemed to still negatively affect others?
3. Is deception ever a good thing?
4. How much do you tell your coworkers or others about an immoral or unethical boss? Is it gossip to warn others?
5. If you have suspicions, should you speak what you believe is the truth or keep your mouth shut?
6. There was a disconnect between what the wise men sought and what Herod was protecting. If you are aware of the spiritual battle all around us, what difference can introducing the kingdom of God in your workplace make?
7. Our morality may be so out of step with the prevailing culture that no one follows. That doesn't mean we are wrong.
8. Knowing that cruelty and violence will continue to happen as long as evil exists, how can we stay positive and seek to be an influence for good?

\*   \*   \*

*"But wisdom is proved right by all her children."*
*(Luke 7:35)*

# Day 20

We Begin with God's Word

Excerpts from Judges 6 & 7

…….The angel of the Lord came and sat down under the oak in Ophrah that belonged to Joash the Abiezrite, where his son Gideon was threshing wheat in a winepress to keep it from the Midianites. When the angel of the Lord appeared to Gideon, he said, "The Lord is with you, mighty warrior."

"Pardon me, my lord," Gideon replied, "but if the Lord is with us, why has all this happened to us? Where are all his wonders that our ancestors told us about when they said, 'Did not the Lord bring us up out of Egypt?' But now the Lord has abandoned us and given us into the hand of Midian." The Lord turned to him and said, "Go in the strength you have and save Israel out of Midian's hand. Am I not sending you?"

"Pardon me, my lord," Gideon replied, "but how can I save Israel? My clan is the weakest in Manasseh, and I am the least in my family."The Lord answered, "I will be with you, and you will strike down all the Midianites, leaving none alive."…….

So Gideon took the men down to the water. There the Lord told him, "Separate those who lap the water with their tongues as a dog laps from those who kneel down to drink." Three hundred of them drank from cupped hands, lapping like dogs. All the rest got down on their knees to drink. The Lord said to Gideon, "With the three hundred men that lapped I will save you and *give the Midianites into your hands. Let all the others go home." So Gideon sent the rest of the Israelites home but kept the three hundred, who took over the provisions and trumpets of the others......*

*Gideon arrived just as a man was telling a friend his dream. "I had a dream," he was saying. "A round loaf of barley bread came tumbling into the Midianite camp. It struck the tent with such force that the tent overturned and collapsed." His friend responded, "This can be nothing other than the sword of Gideon son of Joash, the Israelite. God has given the Midianites and the whole camp into his hands...."*

*They blew their trumpets and broke the jars that were in their hands. The three companies blew the trumpets and smashed the jars. Grasping the torches in their left hands and holding in their right hands the trumpets they were to blow, they shouted, "A sword for the Lord and for Gideon!" While each man held his position around the camp, all the Midianites ran, crying out as they fled...*

# Trumpets and Broken Jars: God's Instruments of Salvation

The Old Testament states fifty-fives times that the Israelites or their king did *"evil in the eyes of the Lord."* And the story following this statement is never good. Kings were deposed or murdered, the people were overrun by their enemies, and Israel often lost its land and God's favor.

By present day standards, some may suggest that this condemnation was a bit harsh. "Who's to say what is evil or what isn't?" The idea of having a general standard of behavior or a baseline for morality and ethics is offensive to those of a more progressive mindset. And yet, a look at the history of our civilization reveals that a set of laws or rules that looks a lot like the Ten Commandments have always been around and generally agreed upon. I support this thesis by the cries of my friends who have lost their jobs due to the evil and corruption of unjust employers. I hear the laments of those who have suffered under the selfishness of those who do not operate by generally agreed upon moral standards.

Gideon was born into a time following 40 years of peace under Deborah. Israel's enemy, the Amalekites, were not so much an invading army as pestering bullies who in no organized fashion would sweep down upon the people and steal their crops and herds and cause confusion and irritation. God heard the cry of the people (as he said he would in the book of Deuteronomy) and appears to Gideon. Was God waiting for this cry? Sometimes it seems to us that God waits too long.

"The Lord is with you, mighty warrior," the angel says to Gideon.  Huh? Who me!?  I doubt Gideon had ever exhibited warrior-like characteristics.  Could it be that the angel saw who Gideon would become rather than who he thought he was?  What does God see in us?

Through a series of miracles, God convinces Gideon that he has a plan.  From a flaming rock to a wet-then-dry fleece. This story is more familiar than most realize as we often hear the colloquialism, *"he put out a fleece"*.  Through it all God patiently develops Gideon's faith and strengthens him as Israel's future leader.

Could Gideon have become a great leader during a time of peace?  Probably not because typically, the great stories come from conflict and deliverance not from peace and tranquility. And the difficulty increases with Gideon's obedience.  He is threatened by his own people when he burns the town's idols.  The ultimate test, however, comes when he was faced with the hordes of Amalekites and his measly army of 32,000.

*"You have too many men,"* God says to Gideon.  In other words, if Gideon attacks with all these warriors, he may take the credit.  So God pares the army down to 300.  Now we're in miracle territory.  But why should we be surprised?   *"What is impossible with man is possible with God"*(Luke 18:27).  Can we look at our adversities as opportunities for God to show up rather than times of defeat?  Could my experience with unemployment make me a better husband and father? Will this time of waiting produce in me patience?  Is it really possible that the enemies in my life are there for my benefit rather than my destruction?

God doesn't leave us in the midst of turmoil and impossibility.  He does what will bring glory to him and be of the most benefit to us. Gideon's warriors are told to pick up trumpets, jars and torches rather than swords, shields and helmets. Doesn't this sound a lot like the Israelites marching around the walls of Jericho? What may seem like nonsense and a waste of time to us are actually God's instruments for our salvation and His honor. The Apostle Paul reminds us that, *"...the foolishness of God is wiser than human wisdom, and the weakness of God is stronger than human strength"(1 Corinthians 1:25).*

To further prove his point, God gives an Amalekite soldier a dream of a huge barley cake rolling into the encampment and wiping out a bunch of soldiers. Certainly not a dream I would have paid attention to but another soldier panics and offers a crazy (but accurate) interpretation: *"This can be nothing other than the sword of Gideon son of Joash, the Israelite. God has given the Midianites and the whole camp into his hands."* Okay...and Gideon got to hear this. It must have made him laugh. A year earlier if you had told Gideon that he would be God's instrument for the deliverance of Israel, he would have been incredulous.

What has God done in our lives in the last year that seemed impossible? What events and circumstances felt insurmountable? We may not be able to control the things that come our way, but we can control our reaction to them. Today, let's blow our trumpets, smash our jars and hold up our torches and put away our swords and shields. Let us practice the faith of Gideon.

Application:
1. What seems like an impossible task for you today?
2. What character traits have I developed in adversity that could not have blossomed in times of ease?

3. Who do you know that could encourage you?
4. Have you ever dismissed an impulse from the Holy Spirit because it seemed silly? Sillier than blowing trumpets and breaking jars?
5. Do you find that you are trusting more in the common sense of people rather than the supernatural Word of God?
6. What can you do today to strengthen your faith?

\* \* \*

When David faced Goliath he said,

*"All those gathered here will know that it is not by sword or spear that the Lord saves; for the battle is the Lord's, and he will give all of you into our hands."*
(1 Samuel 17:47)

# Day 21

We Begin with God's Word

An Excerpt from Judges 11

*Jephthah the Gileadite was a mighty warrior. His father was Gilead; his mother was a prostitute. Gilead's wife also bore him sons, and when they were grown up, they drove Jephthah away. "You are not going to get any inheritance in our family," they said, "because you are the son of another woman." So Jephthah fled from his brothers and settled in the land of Tob, where a gang of scoundrels gathered around him and followed him. Some time later, when the Ammonites were fighting against Israel, the elders of Gilead went to get Jephthah from the land of Tob. "Come," they said, "be our commander, so we can fight the Ammonites..."*

*Then the Spirit of the Lord came on Jephthah. He crossed Gilead and Manasseh, passed through Mizpah of Gilead, and from there he advanced against the Ammonites. And Jephthah made a vow to the Lord: "If you give the Ammonites into my hands, whatever comes out of the door of my house to meet me when I return in triumph from the Ammonites will be the Lord's, and I will sacrifice it as a burnt offering."*

*Then Jephthah went over to fight the Ammonites, and the Lord gave them into his hands. He devastated twenty towns from Aroer to the vicinity of Minnith, as far as Abel Keramim. Thus Israel subdued Ammon. When Jephthah returned to his home in Mizpah, who should come out to meet him but his daughter, dancing to the sound of timbrels! She was an only child. Except for her he had neither son nor daughter. When he saw her, he tore his clothes and cried, "Oh no, my daughter! You have brought me down and I am devastated. I have made a vow to the Lord that I cannot break."*

*"My father," she replied, "you have given your word to the Lord. Do to me just as you promised, now that the Lord has avenged you of your enemies, the Ammonites. But grant me this one request," she said. "Give me two months to roam the hills and weep with my friends, because I will never marry." "You may go," he said. And he let her go for two months. She and her friends went into the hills and wept because she would never marry. After the two months, she returned to her father, and he did to her as he had vowed. And she was a virgin. From this comes the Israelite tradition that each year the young women of Israel go out for four days to commemorate the daughter of Jephthah the Gileadite.*

## Jephthah: Mighty Warrior and Mighty Fool

There are those who believe that if you are born under a particular Zodiac sign you will have such and such a personality. I think most of the descriptions are so general that you could make any one of them apply depending upon the day you are having.

To support a particular point of view, we can find validation in the fact that, when we are born into certain circumstances, our personality will be affected: our birth, country, parents, birth order, health and the socio-economic factors will in some ways determine who we will become.

Jephthah, is said to be the son of Gilead and a prostitute. Not a great beginning for anyone, even then. His brothers later drove him away because they said *"he was the son of another woman."* Jephthah could not help his birth, but he could choose who he would become, just like you and I have a choice. Will he let how he entered the world determine who he will become?

Jephthah became a leader in his own right and when the Ammonites began to threaten Israel, the same people who rejected him called him back to rescue them. Jephthah said to them, *"Didn't you hate me and drive me from my father's house? Why do you come to me now, when you're in trouble?"* The lesson here is that rejection doesn't have to be permanent. Jesus was the *"stone the builders rejected"*, Moses, Joseph, and King David all experienced profound rejection, but in God's wisdom and their obedience, they became renown leaders. Throughout the Old Testament Israel is likened to a prostitute who has thrown herself at neighboring countries and rejected her husband, God, who had freed her from slavery. God says to the prophet Hosea, *"Go, show your love to your wife again, though she is loved by another man and is an adulteress. Love her as the Lord loves the Israelites, though they turn to other gods and love the sacred raisin cakes."* God is faithful even when his people are not.

How ironic that God chooses to save an idolatrous nation by one who was born to a prostitute and rejected by his people. Jephthah steps up and overcomes a victim mentality and the label of his youth, becoming the mighty warrior that Israel needed. God gave Jephthah - and Israel - success. Jephthah experienced the Spirit of God coming upon him and giving him wisdom and strength that were probably supernatural.

Tragically, the story doesn't end well. In his exuberance he said, *"If you give the Ammonites into my hands, whatever comes out of the door of my house to meet me when I return in triumph from the Ammonites will be the Lord's, and I will sacrifice it as a burnt offering."* What occurs next is unfathomable, his daughter greets him when he comes home. This is one of those instances where the words of Scripture are there to show us what *not* to do rather than an example of righteous behavior. His daughter seems to understand her father must keep his vow and asks to spend time with her friends before he fulfills his commitment. I would contend that when a vow is made that is rash, unwise and otherwise foolish, it would be more honorable to repent and remember the nature of our Creator and who He calls us to be.

Application:
1. Do we know our worth despite past failures?

2. Where can we learn our true value if we have suffered loss and rejection? What foundation can we rest upon when worldly success seems to elude us?
3. How are you taking responsibility for your life, despite your circumstances.
4. Remember that if you have been rejected you are in good company.
5. God is sovereign and good. There are times when we need to act, but other times when we just need to wait and watch for him to make a way for you. How can we know the difference?
6. Have you made a foolish promise to someone? Be wise and discerning in determining whether you should fulfill it or not.
7. Where do you find your identity? Our job, friends, health, socio-economic standing are often where we turn. What difference could it make if you found your identity in knowing that God created you, on purpose, for a purpose.

\*   \*   \*

*For you created my inmost being; you knit me together in my mother's womb. I praise you because I am fearfully and wonderfully made; your works are wonderful, I know that full well.*
(Psalm 139:13-14)

# Day 22

We Begin with God's Word

Matthew 3:1-12

*In those days John the Baptist came, preaching in the wilderness of Judea and saying, "Repent, for the kingdom of heaven has come near." This is he who was spoken of through the prophet Isaiah: "A voice of one calling in the wilderness, 'Prepare the way for the Lord, make straight paths for him.'" John's clothes were made of camel's hair, and he had a leather belt around his waist. His food was locusts and wild honey. People went out to him from Jerusalem and all Judea and the whole region of the Jordan. Confessing their sins, they were baptized by him in the Jordan River.*

*But when he saw many of the Pharisees and Sadducees coming to where he was baptizing, he said to them: "You brood of vipers! Who warned you to flee from the coming wrath? Produce fruit in keeping with repentance. And do not think you can say to yourselves, 'We have Abraham as our father.' I tell you that out of these stones God can raise up children for Abraham. The ax is already at the root of the trees, and every tree that does not produce good fruit will be cut down and thrown into the fire.*

*I baptize you with water for repentance. But after me comes one who is more powerful than I, whose sandals I am not worthy to carry. He will baptize you with the Holy Spirit and fire. His winnowing fork is in his hand, and he will clear his threshing floor, gathering his wheat into the barn and burning up the chaff with unquenchable fire."*

# John the Baptist: Entrepreneur and Rabble Rouser

The great thinkers, entrepreneurs, and movers and shakers are often people who struggle socially and have a hard time fitting into society. Steve Jobs, co-founder of Apple, was a difficult man to work with. One early employee wrote, *"He made you feel that you were an important part of something much bigger than yourself — or even bigger than the company. His use of harsh language, humiliation and intimidation were simply hardships to be endured."* And more recently someone who worked with Elon Musk, founder of Tesla and SpaceX, said, *"I highly doubt that there is a cooler company in the world than SpaceX, but if you want a family or hobbies or to see any other aspect of life other than the boundaries of your cubicle, SpaceX is not for you and Elon doesn't seem to give a damn."*

Does it have to be this way? Are we simply to endure the eccentricities of bosses? And what if this describes us?! What should we temper in our personalities in order to *"play well with others"*? What can we learn from John the Baptist, who knew what he was about, understood the importance of his message and sought to honor God above all else?

John the Baptist, as most of the world knows him, was the son of Zechariah a descendant of Aaron, a Levitical priest. In today's language, a "PK", preacher's kid. Raised in the synagogue and temple, he was destined to be someone a bit different because he was born to aging parents who had never had a child. Zechariah had been visited by an angel while offering the yearly sacrifice in the temple and was told that he and his wife would bear a child who would *"make ready a people prepared for the Lord."*

John was different and had a very specific mission, but according to Scripture, God also has specific plans for you and me. Jeremiah 29:11 tells us, *"For I know the plans I have for you,"* declares the Lord, *"plans to prosper you and not to harm you, plans to give you hope and a future."* And Psalm 139:16 says, *"Your eyes saw my unformed body; all the days ordained for me were written in your book before one of them came to be."* There are days when I wonder what my purpose is and I lean heavily upon these truths to bear me up in times of doubt.

John brought a message to a society that should not have been unfamiliar to his hearers…except that he was the first prophet in 400 years. The people of his day resonated with his message of repentance. Being image bearers of God they understood that the path to holiness and a relationship with God was through confession of their sins. But not everyone was onboard. The Pharisees and Sadducees believed their family heritage was enough to place them in good stead with God. They had strayed so far from the truth that God desires obedience, righteousness, and humility.

Therefore, for John to tell them that their genealogy meant nothing and that God could *raise up children of Abraham from rocks* was offensive. John was given a message and evidently a booming voice that could deliver it. But he gave deference to Jesus who had the real message, *"But after me comes one who is more powerful than I, whose sandals I am not worthy to carry. He will baptize you with the Holy Spirit and fire."* The fire of Christ will warm us (remind us of Christ's holiness and comfort following repentance), burn us (drive us to repentance for our sins) or destroy us (when we deny Christ and refuse repentance). Where do I find myself?

The truth is sometimes hard to hear. John seemed to come out of nowhere. And he didn't preach according to the prescribed methods of the Teachers of the Law. God had endowed him with a certain amount of power to bring conviction to the people. But in the final analysis, John was never about himself. He was effective because he delivered God's message. He was powerful because he allowed God to speak through him. He was helpful because he wasted no words and spoke the truth.

Application:
1) Have we discovered the life-giving power of repentance, coming clean of known sin and wrong doing?
2) If we were rebuked by a John the Baptist, how would we respond?
3) If we have been endowed with a certain power (personality, authority, position), have we used it to serve others or for selfish gain?
4) How can we be true to ourselves, speak truth and yet make a living?
5) Being a natural child of Abraham meant that you were connected to the lineage of God's chosen people. Yet, John discounts this. What is John's message to you today?

\*     \*     \*

*Do not conform to the pattern of this world, but be transformed by the renewing of your mind. Then you will be able to test and approve what God's will is—*

*his good, pleasing and perfect will.*
                                    (Romans 12:2)

# Day 23

We Begin with God's Word

Excerpts from the Book of Ruth

## Chapter 1

*…But Naomi said, "Return home, my daughters. Why would you come with me? Am I going to have any more sons, who could become your husbands? Return home, my daughters; I am too old to have another husband. Even if I thought there was still hope for me— even if I had a husband tonight and then gave birth to sons— would you wait until they grew up? Would you remain unmarried for them? No, my daughters. It is more bitter for me than for you, because the Lord's hand has turned against me!"…*

*But Ruth replied, "Don't urge me to leave you or to turn back from you. Where you go I will go, and where you stay I will stay. Your people will be my people and your God my God. Where you die I will die, and there I will be buried. May the Lord deal with me, be it ever so severely, if even death separates you and me."…*

## Chapter 2

*…Boaz replied, "I've been told all about what you have done for your mother-in-law since the death of your husband—how you left your father and mother and your homeland and came to live with a people you did not know before. May the Lord repay you for what you have done. May you be richly rewarded by the Lord, the God of Israel, under whose wings you have come to take refuge."…*

## Chapter 3

…"The Lord bless you, my daughter," he replied. "This kindness is greater than that which you showed earlier: You have not run after the younger men, whether rich or poor. And now, my daughter, don't be afraid. I will do for you all you ask. All the people of my town know that you are a woman of noble character. Although it is true that I am a guardian-redeemer of our family, there is another who is more closely related than I. Stay here for the night, and in the morning if he wants to do his duty as your guardian-redeemer, good; let him redeem you. But if he is not willing, as surely as the Lord lives I will do it. Lie here until morning…"

## Chapter 4

…So Boaz took Ruth and she became his wife. When he made love to her, the Lord enabled her to conceive, and she gave birth to a son. The women said to Naomi: "Praise be to the Lord, who this day has not left you without a guardian-redeemer. May he become famous throughout Israel! He will renew your life and sustain you in your old age. For your daughter-in-law, who loves you and who is better to you than seven sons, has given him birth."…

# Ruth: A Woman of Character

How do we behave when all that is familiar is stripped from us? Being in a foreign country can often leave us feeling that our values and traditions have no place. As a prisoner of war, Louis Zamperini was challenged on all fronts to surrender his values, character and integrity. He survived in a raft for 47 days after his bomber crash-landed in the ocean during the Second World War and then was sent to prisoner of war camps. "Unbroken" is the movie about his experience and how he refused to cooperate with his captors to broadcast anti-American propaganda or be humiliated by Watanabe, the Japanese corporal in charge of the camp.

Chapter 1: Tragedy Reveals Our Loyalty

In the Old Testament book of Ruth, we enter a time of famine and tragedy. Naomi had lost her husband and two sons. Like Louis Zamperini, she was faced with unthinkable odds. She and her two daughters-in-law had to make a choice: stay in the land of Moab or return to Naomi's home, Israel. Orpah, at Naomi's urging stayed but Ruth was unmoved. She tells Naomi, *"Don't urge me to leave you or to turn back from you. Where you go I will go, and where you stay I will stay. Your people will be my people and your God my God. Where you die I will die, and there I will be buried. May the Lord deal with me, be it ever so severely, if even death separates you and me."*

Do we judge Ruth as foolish and reckless, or is she a role model, demonstrating character that will be proven to be solid and true? Naomi relented and the two of them entered Bethlehem, where Ruth observed her mother-in-law in this new land. She must have been surprised at the reaction of the people to the apparent wear-and-tear life had had on Naomi as they remark, *"Can this be Naomi?"*

Chapter 2: Our Character Is Formed in Difficult Times

Ruth does not wait for Naomi to provide for her but quickly initiated by gleaning in a nearby field. A practice provided by God in the Law for the poor. Leviticus 19:10 states, *"Do not go over your vineyard a second time or pick up the grapes that have fallen. Leave them for the poor and the foreigner."* A sign that Naomi must have discipled Ruth in the Law of her people. In God's sovereignty, *"she was working in a field belonging to Boaz."* This was the land of Naomi's relative. A good sign for an Israelite considering their deep devotion to family.

It can be humiliating to stoop to menial labor in a time of need, but we see Ruth as a model of behavior, *"She came into the field and has remained here from morning till now, except for a short rest in the shelter."* Maybe unknowingly, Ruth was representing a righteous woman, what it meant to be a daughter-in-law, a widow and a Moabite. With each action we signal to the world to whom we are loyal and how one who believes as we do behaves.

Chapter 3: Trusting Godly Advice

Although God is sovereign we still need to act. Ruth submits to Naomi who knew the culture of the land and followed her instructions. The beauty of this partnership is that each was looking out for the other. Ruth provided for their daily needs through her hard work and Naomi looked out for Ruth's future by seeking out her kinsman redeemer - the nearest male relative who had the privilege or responsibility to act on behalf of a relative who was in trouble, danger, or need.

Naomi instructed Ruth in the following way after the work was done that day, *"When he lies down, note the place where he is lying. Then go and uncover his feet and lie down. He will tell you what to do."* Since we don't understand the culture of the day, Ruth's actions seem somewhat promiscuous and seen through the lens of modern times we may wonder if she compromised herself. Knowing her behavior up to this point, I am willing to give her the benefit of the doubt and trust that the culture provided for Naomi's proactive plan. A commentator notes that *Ruth lay at Boaz's feet, not by his side.* This episode also demonstrated that each actor in this drama was concerned for the other's integrity and within the allowances of the culture's best practices.

## Chapter 4: Leave the Result to God

Now let's wait and see what happens. Naomi even says to Ruth, *"Wait, my daughter, until you find out what happens. For the man will not rest until the matter is settled today."* She trusted Boaz and she trusted God. The story concluded with Boaz negotiating with a nearer kinsman redeemer than he and we must admire the end result from the perspective of both. The winner of the bargain would not only inherit the family's land but also Ruth. Land is one thing...but a woman along with the deal? Boaz's opponent stated, *"Then I cannot redeem it because I might endanger my own estate."* I think he meant, my wife would not appreciate the bonus included with the deal.

Boaz gladly accepted the responsibility of Ruth and Naomi's land. A good ending is always satisfying but a full view of the context reveals how God cares for his people and provides for all their needs. Boaz was the son of Rahab the harlot of the defeated town of Jericho in the days of Joshua. When Boaz marries Ruth, a Moabite, they have a child named Obed who becomes the father of Jesse whose son is David. Little did we know that when this story began, that God was weaving, from many nations, the family line that would produce our Messiah. As Paul Harvey, a radio commentator years ago used to say, *"Now you know....the REST of the story."*

Application:
1. In a time of tragedy, to whom will you be devoted?
2. Does hard work and loyalty always pay off? Is it important anyway?
3. Ruth sought to be a blessing to Naomi. Are we a blessing to everyone with whom we come in contact?
4. How does our behavior and character bless previous and future generations?
5. What are the benefits or consequences if we do the right thing even if we don't see the immediate outcome?
6. How well do we represent our people, our country or our company?
7. Are we willing like Ruth to do whatever it takes to make a living?
8. What rules have you had to obey that you didn't understand at first?
9. At the end of the day, ask yourself "Who have I blessed? What good work have I accomplished? Have I left anything undone?"
10. Regardless of our socio-economic status, should our values and ethics be the same?

\* \* \*

*In love a throne will be established; in faithfulness a man will sit on it— one from the house of David— one who in judging seeks justice and speeds the cause of righteousness.*
(Isaiah 16:5)

# Day 24

We Begin with God's Word

John 2:1-12

*On the third day a wedding took place at Cana in Galilee. Jesus' mother was there, and Jesus and his disciples had also been invited to the wedding. When the wine was gone, Jesus' mother said to him, "They have no more wine." "Woman, why do you involve me?" Jesus replied. "My hour has not yet come." His mother said to the servants, "Do whatever he tells you."*

*Nearby stood six stone water jars, the kind used by the Jews for ceremonial washing, each holding from twenty to thirty gallons. Jesus said to the servants, "Fill the jars with water"; so they filled them to the brim. Then he told them, "Now draw some out and take it to the master of the banquet." They did so, and the master of the banquet tasted the water that had been turned into wine. He did not realize where it had come from, though the servants who had drawn the water knew.*

*Then he called the bridegroom aside and said, "Everyone brings out the choice wine first and then the cheaper wine after the guests have had too much to drink; but you have saved the best till now." What Jesus did here in Cana of Galilee was the first of the signs through which he revealed his glory; and his disciples believed in him. After this he went down to Capernaum with his mother and brothers and his disciples. There they stayed for a few days.*

# Jesus: Would You Invite Him to Your Company Party?

The company party has a rather unsavory reputation. The culprit is most often the abuse of alcohol. The attraction of strong drink is that it enables a person to relax, subdues the inhibitions and gives you something to do while engaging in what is often uncomfortable conversation. The downside is that some relax too much, too many inhibitions are released and words are said that can never be taken back.

With this cultural framework in mind we may approach this passage with some skepticism as we discover that the multiplication of alcohol was Jesus' first miracle. Many would agree with the Pharisees, *"Here is a glutton and a drunkard, a friend of tax collectors and sinners."* But the Pharisees had a double standard. They didn't like John the Baptist either, *"For John came neither eating nor drinking, and they say, 'He has a demon."* Make up your mind, will you?!

Jesus is about thirty years old when he performs his first miracle. He and his disciples (only 5 at this time) were invited to a wedding, and we can assume that based on his socio-economic status, that these friends were not wealthy. It may have been a financial stretch to have so many guests to a small affair such as this. So, when they ran out of wine, it may have been their fault. Jesus' mother says to him, *"They have no more wine"*. This could mean one of several things: 1) Your five disciples drank too much, 2) Could you go out and get some more, or as most people seem to think, 3) Do something miraculous and fix the situation. But she could merely have been trusting that Jesus would politely apologize for the shortfall to the party goers and protect the reputation of the wedding couple.

This is where we begin to get a glimpse of the character of the Son of God. There was nothing wrong with Mary wanting him to fix the situation. It's sort of like when we ask God to do what he thinks is best. Jesus does not draw attention to himself or make a public announcement declaring that he will indeed take care of things. He quietly asks the servants to fill the available jars with water. (Water was always available for foot washing, ceremonial washing and general cleaning.) And he doesn't wave his hand dramatically over the jars saying *"Abracadabra!'* He merely directs the servants to take it to the master of the banquet. Shouldn't Jesus have tried it first to make sure it tasted alright? He doesn't have to. If this is Messiah, the Son of God, the great *I am*, then as creator of the universe, he can easily create wine and, as Genesis 1 declares about everything he created, *"it was good"*.

Only the servants and the disciples knew that it was Jesus who had done a miracle. Jesus protected the reputation of the couple at the most important event in their married life. The master of the banquet was impressed by this young couple's ability to do what was counter cultural…to provide the best wine toward the end of the banquet. Jesus honored his mother by taking care of the situation in a way that probably surprised her. And the disciples had seen enough to put their faith in him.

Application:
1) Like Mary, make your requests to Jesus and leave the results to him.
2) Serve your family or your company with humility. Seek to enhance the reputation of others by

serving them.  When we serve others we practice Matthew 6:33, *"But seek first his kingdom and his righteousness, and all these things will be given to you as well."*

3) Seek to benefit your company through quiet service, honest hard work and a self-deprecating attitude.

4) Enjoy seeing others praised even if they get credit for something you did.

5) Work for the benefit of your company trusting that God will reward you for your hard work even if you are not recognized.

6) We practice the fruit of the Spirit. Galatians 5:22,23 *"...which is love, joy, peace, forbearance, kindness, goodness, faithfulness, gentleness and self-control. Against such things there is no law."*

7) We give people the benefit of the doubt. 1 Corinthians 10:23,24  *"I have the right to do anything," you say—but not everything is beneficial. "I have the right to do anything"—but not everything is constructive. No one should seek their own good, but the good of others."*

\*     \*     \*

*Whatever you do, work at it with all your heart,*
*as working for the Lord, not for human masters.*
(Colossians 3:23)

# Day 25

We Begin with God's Word

Mark 10:17-31

*As Jesus started on his way, a man ran up to him and fell on his knees before him. "Good teacher," he asked, "what must I do to inherit eternal life?" "Why do you call me good?" Jesus answered. "No one is good—except God alone. You know the commandments: 'You shall not murder, you shall not commit adultery, you shall not steal, you shall not give false testimony, you shall not defraud, honor your father and mother.'"*

*"Teacher," he declared, "all these I have kept since I was a boy." Jesus looked at him and loved him. "One thing you lack," he said. "Go, sell everything you have and give to the poor, and you will have treasure in heaven. Then come, follow me." At this the man's face fell. He went away sad, because he had great wealth. Jesus looked around and said to his disciples, "How hard it is for the rich to enter the kingdom of God!"*
*The disciples were amazed at his words. But Jesus said again, "Children, how hard it is to enter the kingdom of God! It is easier for a camel to go through the eye of a needle than for someone who is rich to enter the kingdom of God." The disciples were even more amazed, and said to each other, "Who then can be saved?" Jesus looked at them and said, "With man this is impossible, but not with God; all things are possible with God."*

*Then Peter spoke up, "We have left everything to follow you!" "Truly I tell you," Jesus replied, "no one who has left home or brothers or sisters or mother or father or children or fields for me and the gospel will fail to receive a hundred times as much in this present age: homes, brothers, sisters, mothers, children and fields— along with persecutions—and in the age to come eternal life. But many who are first will be last, and the last first."*

# Jesus: The Ideal Boss

Justin Sun, the 28-year-old founder of blockchain platform TRON and CEO of peer-to-peer file sharing protocol BitTorrent, won the annual eBay charity auction to have lunch with Warren Buffett at the steakhouse Smith & Wollensky in New York City. For only $4.6 million. What would you pay to have lunch with a powerful and influential person? Not many of us can compete in this realm but we all have dreams of meeting someone famous and having the opportunity to get to know them.

In today's passage, a young man boldly asked Jesus a question that at one time or another we may want to ask, *"Good teacher what must I do to inherit eternal life?"* The translation could be any one of the following: *"How much can I get away with and still be allowed through the pearly gates?"* *"How much good is really required?"* Or as the Pharisees in the first century used to argue, *"Which is the greatest commandment and therefore the most important one to obey?"*

Jesus deflected the question entirely and focused on the word "good". The ancient Jewish understanding of "good" was not the way we use it: "good" was equivalent to our "great". Therefore, the honor this man was paying to Jesus lifted him to the highest status. This passage is full of implications for our lives! Let's focus on five main points:

### 1) Jesus tells us the truth

We live in a world where truth is relative. But according to Scripture there are absolute truths, and they can set us free. Jesus saw through this man's question and got to the heart of the matter. He asked him about his obedience to the Ten Commandments and if he had obeyed a few of them. Interestingly, Jesus only asked him about the ones that deal with our interpersonal relationships. Outwardly, most of us could agree and say that we too, have obeyed them. Jesus didn't argue. But He dove deeper. *"One thing you lack," he said. "Go, sell everything you have and give to the poor, and you will have treasure in heaven. Then come, follow me."*

The heart of the matter was the man's idolatry. It's the one thing we may lack as well. We often place career, money, people, fashion, vanity or possessions ahead of our devotion to God. Are we willing to accept this truth?

### 2) Jesus corrects our distorted thinking

The truth is the young man had not kept all the commandments. And neither have we. But somehow Jesus knew that arguing with him would not accomplish anything. Instead he hit the young man where it hurt. Jesus knew that money and possessions were at the center of his life. Jesus essentially said, *'That is no way to live. You can't just add me to your already busy and cluttered life. To really live I need your whole-hearted devotion. Are you willing to give it all up and follow me?'* It's only when we get to this point do we truly begin to understand biblical Christianity.

### 3) A kingdom of God mindset

*"Children, how hard it is to enter the kingdom of God! It is easier for a camel to go through the eye of a needle than for someone who is rich to enter the*

*kingdom of God."* Huh?! The disciples got it right when they asked, *"Who then can be saved?"* Jesus made it clear that no human path can lead to heaven. No amount of good works, holy living, church-going, charity, piety, etc. will ever do us any good. Until we get to the point where we see the impossibility of jumping the chasm from our way of thinking to his, do we have an inkling of hope.

### 4) Jesus is in charge

Are we ready to concede that we do not have it all under control? Are we ready to stop making foolish assumptions that we can do anything "good" apart from God? The most offensive part of this story was that Jesus defined the ground rules. He acted like he was actually in charge of who goes to heaven and who doesn't. He even defined the meaning of success. Who gets to do that? That's what offended people then so much. Only God can forgive sins. And only God has the right to tell us how to live in this world. C.S. Lewis had it right when he said, *"You must make your choice: either this man was, and is, the Son of God, or else a madman or something worse. You can shut him up for a fool, you can spit at him and kill him as a demon; or you can fall at his feet and call him Lord and God. But let us not come with any patronizing nonsense about his being a great human teacher. He has not left that open to us. He did not intend to."*

### 5) Nobody bargains with God

There's a difference between humility and being patronizing. The young man was not willing to humble himself before Jesus. He was merely trying to see what he could get away with. Many of us have lived upright lives in the eyes of the people around us.

However, man-made rules are illusions. We actually live according to the laws of the universe, that is, God's rules. God cannot be bribed or patronized. Neither will he demand that you pay $4.5 million to have lunch with him. The gift of eternal life is free - but it will cost you everything you have. To enter the kingdom of God, Jesus says that *"we must deny ourselves, take up cross daily in order to follow him."*

The good news is that *"Jesus looked at him and loved him."* This is good news because he looks at us in the same way. C.S. Lewis in his book, The Screwtape Letters, has a statement made by the chief demon, *"For we must never forget the most repellent and inexplicable trait in our Enemy[God]; He really loves the hairless bipeds He has created..."*

The truth of God's love for us is demonstrated by the very air we breathe, all the way to the salvation he offers us through Jesus' death on the cross. The following principles reveal that it is possible to live successful lives on this earth and thrive, whether I am gainfully employed or wondering where my next meal will come from?

Application:
1. God loves us. We ought to view everything through this lens. How does this affect how we view the people and circumstances in our life?
2. In a world where truth is perceived as relative, the Bible gives us absolute principles that are true for all people, in all places, at all times.
3. To be successful on this earth, a kingdom of God mindset is needed in order to interpret the events of our day. Otherwise, we are subject to the whims of our imagination.

4. If Jesus is in charge then we are free to fail, free to take risks, free to pursue his view of life regardless of the consequences.
5. We must face life on God's terms. Will we willingly submit to him and agree with him?

\*   \*   \*

*"Seek first his kingdom and his righteousness, and all these things will be given to you as well."*
(Matthew 6:33)

# Day 26

We Begin With God's Word

Luke 9:21-27

*Jesus strictly warned them not to tell this [that he was the Messiah] to anyone. And he said, "The Son of Man must suffer many things and be rejected by the elders, the chief priests and the teachers of the law, and he must be killed and on the third day be raised to life." Then he said to them all: "Whoever wants to be my disciple must deny themselves and take up their cross daily and follow me. For whoever wants to save their life will lose it, but whoever loses their life for me will save it. What good is it for someone to gain the whole world, and yet lose or forfeit their very self? Whoever is ashamed of me and my words, the Son of Man will be ashamed of them when he comes in his glory and in the glory of the Father and of the holy angels. "Truly I tell you, some who are standing here will not taste death before they see the kingdom of God."*

## Jesus: The Ideal Employee

What do Pastor Lee Jong-rak, Rick Rescorla, and Dr. Megan Coffee have in common?  For starters, I've never heard of any of them. Secondly, they did something amazing that affected many lives.  In South Korea Pastor Lee took in mentally handicapped and unwanted babies to stop them from being abandoned on the side of the road.  Rick Rescorla was the security director for Morgan Stanley who helped all but 13 of Morgan Stanley's 2,700 employees escape on 9/11. Dr. Coffee is a specialist in infectious diseases who has been working in Haiti since the earthquake in 2010, without pay.

What recognition do we need to stay in our current job?  Or what do we think we need in order to thrive and grow in our particular situation?  The message of the world around us is to seek every advantage for yourself, you can do anything if you put your mind to it and follow your passions. Biblical Christianity tells us to seek first the kingdom of God, strive for excellence for the sake of others, do what God has equipped you to do and follow Jesus Christ at all costs.

Jesus said, *"For whoever wants to save their life will lose it, but whoever loses their life for me will save it."* Could it be that the saving of our lives, though a natural function, must be denied and the losing of our lives, is an unnatural function must be desired?  If this is true, the follower of Christ will be following a very different set of principles, but ones that will in the long run bring the most satisfaction...but not without consequence.

Pastor Lee gave up his own comfort to serve those who are destitute.  Mr. Rescorla could have died by staying longer than was safe. Dr. Coffee, with her talent and skill, certainly could have attained notoriety in the U.S. What do they understand about meaning in this life that many of us do not?

Having been involved in the job-seeking world, I have seen at least two paths that the unemployed take: 1) self-pity, anger, bitterness and blame or 2) humility, acceptance and a genuine desire to help others in the same situation. Fortunately, some who start down the first path end up in the second. I contend that those who have suffered from unemployment and financial stress are the most compassionate, wise, and helpful toward others in need. It is true that periods of deprivation make us more appreciative of the little that we do have.

But does it work? Does this life of self denial and following principles that are completely other-centered lead to a more satisfying life? What is Jesus talking about when he refers to losing our soul? Do our day-to-day decisions really make a difference for eternity?

We do not need to wait for the life here-after to find out the answers to these questions. Just like the three people I mentioned, we can evaluate whether the lives we have chosen are worthwhile. We certainly have at our fingertips countless stories of sacrifice. And, as I mentioned, I have watched many come through our job seeking network and learn principles of job hunting that help not only themselves but others along the way.

I just read a book where the author argues that in order to be "successful" one must be fiercely independent. This definition would have to imply the using of others for your betterment. Not a great way to "win friends and influence people." So, as I'm thinking about my many friends looking for satisfying work, I would like to suggest the following:

Application:
1) Do an experiment, a cost-benefit analysis.
   a. Intentionally put others first. Look for opportunities to serve. Be available for others.
   b. Intentionally be selfish. Avoid situations that require service. Be first whenever possible.
2) Examine the life of Christ by reading the Gospels. Who were his friends and enemies? What kinds of people were attracted to him and who were repulsed?
3) Reflect on your own work history. Have you been most satisfied in a culture where people served each other in a sacrificial way or one where each was only concerned for themselves?
4) If you are a follower of Jesus Christ recognize that you bring the kingdom of God with you wherever you go. The power of the Holy Spirit flows through you to transform any situation by enabling you to serve beyond what you thought you were capable.
5) Following Christ's principles in your job will bring about the kind of success that will last and bring the most satisfaction.

\*   \*   \*

*But seek first his kingdom and his righteousness,*
*and all these things will be given to you as well.*
*Matthew 6:33*

# Day 27

We Begin with God's Word

John 3:1-21

*Now there was a Pharisee, a man named Nicodemus who was a member of the Jewish ruling council. He came to Jesus at night and said, "Rabbi, we know that you are a teacher who has come from God. For no one could perform the signs you are doing if God were not with him." Jesus replied, "Very truly I tell you, no one can see the kingdom of God unless they are born again." "How can someone be born when they are old?" Nicodemus asked. "Surely they cannot enter a second time into their mother's womb to be born!"*

*Jesus answered, "Very truly I tell you, no one can enter the kingdom of God unless they are born of water and the Spirit. Flesh gives birth to flesh, but the Spirit gives birth to spirit. You should not be surprised at my saying, 'You must be born again.' The wind blows wherever it pleases. You hear its sound, but you cannot tell where it comes from or where it is going. So it is with everyone born of the Spirit." "How can this be?" Nicodemus asked. "You are Israel's teacher," said Jesus, "and do you not understand these things? Very truly I tell you, we speak of what we know, and we testify to what we have seen, but still you people do not accept our testimony. I have spoken to you of earthly things and you do not believe; how then will you believe if I speak of heavenly things?*

*No one has ever gone into heaven except the one who came from heaven—the Son of Man. Just as Moses lifted up the snake in the wilderness, so the Son of Man must be lifted up, that everyone who believes may have eternal life in him." For God so loved the world that he gave his one and only Son, that whoever believes in him shall not perish but have eternal life. For God did not send his Son into the world to condemn the world, but to save the world through him. Whoever believes in him is not condemned, but whoever does not believe stands condemned already because they have not believed in the name of God's one and only Son.*

*This is the verdict: Light has come into the world, but people loved darkness instead of light because their deeds were evil. Everyone who does evil hates the light, and will not come into the light for fear that their deeds will be exposed. But whoever lives by the truth comes into the light, so that it may be seen plainly that what they have done has been done in the sight of God.*

## Jesus: Company Policy

"Why is this sale item displayed like this," asked the new sales associate, "I disagree with this merchandising practice."  "Because this is what we were told by Corporate," said the manager.  Is there a way to respectfully question company practices without being rude and impertinent?  And in the end what should the response of the newly hired sales associate be?  Compliance will guarantee future employment whereas ill-timed and rude questioning may result in termination or in the least, getting off on the wrong foot.

In this Scripture passage, Nicodemus questioned Jesus either as one was genuinely curious or as one who presumed to think that he could corner Jesus on an obscure Jewish text.  But Jesus preempted him and took him down what should have been a familiar road.  He reminded Nicodemus of God's company policy.  Nicodemus was baffled because the Jews had deviated from the truth of God's Law and created a works-oriented system in which true compliance was impossible.

Adherence to God's Law was never intended to bring life but merely to point to the ONE who can give life. The Apostle Paul lamented in the letter to the Romans how futile it is to depend upon the Law as a producer of righteousness and admits his struggle by concluding with *Romans 7:24,25 "What a wretched man I am! Who will rescue me from this body that is subject to death? Thanks be to God, who delivers me through Jesus Christ our Lord!"*

So, If Nicodemus was headed down one path and Jesus another, what does Jesus want him to understand about a biblical understanding of salvation? In other words, what is Heaven's company policy? Nicodemus was coming from the perspective that perfect adherence to the Law of Moses was what was required. Although, he probably knew it was impossible, he hoped, as many people do today, that his good works would outweigh his bad and that God would look upon him with favor. But there was no security, no assurance and certainly no peace with God.

Jesus turned things inside out and reminded Nicodemus of the essence of the Law. *You must be born again."* You need to start over, you can't bring anything with you, it's as if you are entering this relationship as a baby, with nothing. The central point Jesus made was in *verse 16, "For God so loved the world that he gave his one and only Son, that whoever believes in him shall not perish but have eternal life."* It is God who has done all the work. All you need to do is believe. But it's clear that some will be let in and some will be left out. A policy that is unpopular among many today.

But there were some in Jesus day that understood this policy. When Jesus had entered Capernaum, a centurion came to him, asking for help. *"Lord," he said, "my servant lies at home paralyzed, suffering terribly." Jesus said to him, "Shall I come and heal him?" The centurion replied, "Lord, I do not deserve to have you come under my roof. But just say the word, and my servant will be healed. For I myself am a man under authority, with soldiers under me. I tell this one, 'Go,' and he goes; and that one, 'Come,' and he comes. I say to my servant, 'Do this,' and he does it." When Jesus heard this, he was amazed and said to those following him, "Truly I tell you, I have not found anyone in Israel with such great faith." [Matthew 8:6-10]*

What did the centurion believe? That Jesus had the power to do anything? Is faith that simple? Is Heaven's company policy that clear cut? To follow Christ is not simply to have a religious aspect to my life but it permeates every nook and cranny so that a disciple of Christ makes the best friend, spouse, and certainly employee or boss. One who knows Jesus' company policy has an understanding of submission, compliance, patience and authority that applies to every area of our existence. Let's follow his example by doing three things: Have a humble approach to Jesus, recognize His authority and submit to His approach to life.

Application:
1) Submission to company policy has its root in biblical principles. We're able to obey in our present circumstances because we have a biblical and global perspective.
2) Heaven's company policy has direct application to living in today's world. How we view God, life and work makes the follower of Christ the best employee.
3) Ask questions, question authority with respect, but be ready to submit as a sign of maturity and faith.
4) We are all under authority. Practice submission with respect in cooperation with those under, equal to, and over you for the greater good.
5) Consider, like Nicodemus, that your world view is skewed. If you are having problems with human relationships, then it may be that your understanding of Heaven's company policy needs realignment.

*   *   *

*As Jesus went on from there, he saw a man named Matthew sitting at the tax collector's booth. "Follow me," he told him, and Matthew got up and followed him.*

(Matthew 9:9)

# Day 28

We Begin with God's Word

Excerpts from John 4

*...So Jesus left Judea and went back once more to Galilee. Now he had to go through Samaria. Jacob's well was there, and Jesus, tired as he was from the journey, sat down by the well. It was about noon. When a Samaritan woman came to draw water, Jesus said to her, "Will you give me a drink?"*

*The Samaritan woman said to him, "You are a Jew and I am a Samaritan woman. How can you ask me for a drink?" (For Jews do not associate with Samaritans.) Jesus answered her, "If you knew the gift of God and who it is that asks you for a drink, you would have asked him and he would have given you living water." "Sir," the woman said, "you have nothing to draw with and the well is deep. Where can you get this living water? Are you greater than our father Jacob, who gave us the well and drank from it himself, as did also his sons and his livestock?" Jesus answered, "Everyone who drinks this water will be thirsty again, but whoever drinks the water I give them will never thirst. Indeed, the water I give them will become in them a spring of water welling up to eternal life."*

*The woman said to him, "Sir, give me this water so that I won't get thirsty and have to keep coming here to draw water." He told her, "Go, call your husband and come back." "I have no husband," she replied. Jesus said to her, "You are right when you say you have no husband. The fact is, you have had five husbands, and the man you now have is not your husband. What you have just said is quite true." "Sir," the woman said, "I can see that you are a prophet. Our ancestors worshiped on this mountain, but you Jews claim that the place where we must worship is in Jerusalem." "Woman," Jesus replied, "believe me, a time is coming when you will worship the Father neither on this mountain nor in Jerusalem. You Samaritans worship what you do not know; we worship what we do know, for salvation is from the Jews. Yet a time is coming and has now come when the true worshipers will worship the Father in the Spirit and in truth, for they are the kind of worshipers the Father seeks. God is spirit, and his worshipers must worship in the Spirit and in truth."*

*The woman said, "I know that Messiah" (called Christ) "is coming. When he comes, he will explain everything to us." Then Jesus declared, "I, the one speaking to you—I am he." Just then his disciples returned and were surprised to find him talking with a woman. Then, leaving her water jar, the woman went back to the town and said to the people, "Come, see a man who told me everything I ever did. Could this be the Messiah?"*

*…Many of the Samaritans from that town believed in him because of the woman's testimony, "He told me everything I ever did." And because of his words many more became believers. They said to the woman, "We no longer believe just because of what you said; now we have heard for ourselves, and we know that this man really is the Savior of the world."*

## Jesus: Equal Pay for Equal Work

On June 10, 1963 President John F. Kennedy's <u>Equal Pay Act</u> was signed into law with the express purpose of ensuring that women got paid equally for equal work. And yet today we continue to argue over what that means. Sweden, Finland, Denmark and Norway are near the top in the world when it comes to gender equality in the workplace. This is demonstrated by equal pay and equal maternity leave.

In our present day culture, sexual differences are being distorted. On the one hand modern science is ignoring biology, and on the other, an attempt is being made at achieving a neuter sex. But wonderful and beautiful differences exist between us that make this world not only livable but interesting and vibrant. The Bible says in *Genesis 1:27 says, "So God created mankind in his own image, in the image of God he created them; male and female he created them."* In other words, communities are not complete without a mix of male and female, where each sex is able to express their uniqueness in the ways our Creator intended.

An accurate reading of Scripture will reveal a God who we know as a loving father and primarily men who have received His revelation. And yet there are differences in the way a biblical follower of Christ acts, based on the knowledge of how we are made and most importantly through the example of Jesus Christ. In the story of Jesus meeting the Samaritan woman at the well, a cultural shake-up occurred that a cursory reading of the passage does not reveal.

We are first amazed that Jesus and his disciples went through Samaria at all. Jews, in that day, would walk ten to fifteen miles out of their way in order to avoid these half-breed people.  The Samaritans had Jewish heritage but it had been mixed hundreds of years before and those who thought they were pure-bred Jews (although there's no such thing - see the genealogy in Matthew 1) despised them.  Secondly, Jesus approached the well in the heat of the day when most women would not have been there.  Only the Samaritan woman, a woman of some ill-repute, came when she would not have to endure the ridicule of the other villagers.

Jesus then crossed another cultural divide by actually speaking to her.  Any Jewish man of standing and especially a Rabbi would not only not speak to woman in public and certainly not to a Samaritan one.  What was he thinking?   It's as if Jesus' entrance into our universe offered a corrective to our distorted mindsets.  The conversation between the two of them quickly dove deep into the essential meaning of life.  What a gift!  To be able to cut through the small talk and speak about the things that really matter.

They go back and forth discussing physical water and spiritual water.  Jesus corrected her thinking about the Messiah and his origin.  Again, Jesus tactfully and effectively heard her objections and took the conversation exactly where it should have gone….to the state of her soul.  This was revealed when he was able to see into the woman's checkered past and expose her empty way of life. *"You are right when you say you have no husband. The fact is, you have had five husbands, and the man you now have is not your husband."*

The woman had a choice at this moment: 1) Run away in a huff at this stranger's impudence, 2) Loudly declare her innocence….in the movies this is where the woman usually slaps the man across the face or 3) Humbly accept his loving judgment and find out what's behind his line of questioning.  It seemed that she went with #3 because she wanted to know more about Jesus.

Beginning at verse 21 Jesus exposed the weaknesses in human religion.  Jews do it one way, Samaritans another.  But the point is, God is above all that.  Verse 24 says *"God is spirit, and his worshipers must worship in the Spirit and in truth."*  He didn't say men worshipers but all people.  In other words, the whole point of this conversation is that God has revealed from the beginning of time, through Scripture, and now through Jesus, that he wants to bring men and women into a relationship with him.  The path for both is equal.  Each of us needs to submit to our Creator, drink the living water, repent of our past behavior and allow him to transform our lives.  We are all equal in our need.

This is Jesus' way.  Yes, he chose twelve men to be his disciples but he employed many women to be evangelists as well.  This Samaritan woman being one of the first,  for she went back to her village and said, *"Come, see a man who told me everything I ever did. Could this be the Messiah?" They came out of the town and made their way toward him."*

Was it a risk for Jesus to talk with her?  Absolutely!  The Scriptures say,  *"Just then his disciples returned and were surprised to find him talking with a woman. But no one asked, "What do you want?" or "Why are you talking with her?""*  I wonder why Peter was silent at this point.  That's not like him.  And Judas, he was quite opinionated as well.  Maybe they were so stunned as to be speechless.

The result of this encounter is undeniable. *The women's friends told her, "We no longer believe just because of what you said; now we have heard for ourselves, and we know that this man really is the Savior of the world."* It's clear that much good came from the risk that Jesus took. Could this story have implications for us in our interactions with other people?

Application:
1) Are you willing to examine yourself to see what wrong cultural practices and prejudices you continue to carry?
2) With the world's attempt to bring equality how does Jesus' approach differ and why is it successful?
3) What difference would it make in the workplace if men and women were treated equally?
4) What will you do today to communicate your understanding of equality in your interaction with people?
5) Who do you need to apologize to for your unfair treatment? This could go back years, but as the Psalmist declares many times, *"Confession is good for the soul".* When we understand that we are forgiven in Jesus Christ, then we can forgive others.

\* \* \*

*Among the gods there is none like you, Lord; no deeds can compare with yours. All the nations you have made will come and worship before you, Lord; they will bring glory to your name.*
(Psalm 86:8,9)

# Day 29

We Begin with God's Word

John 6:16-30

*When evening came, his disciples went down to the lake, where they got into a boat and set off across the lake for Capernaum. By now it was dark, and Jesus had not yet joined them. A strong wind was blowing and the waters grew rough. When they had rowed about three or four miles, they saw Jesus approaching the boat, walking on the water; and they were frightened. But he said to them, "It is I; don't be afraid." Then they were willing to take him into the boat, and immediately the boat reached the shore where they were heading.*

*The next day the crowd that had stayed on the opposite shore of the lake realized that only one boat had been there, and that Jesus had not entered it with his disciples, but that they had gone away alone. Then some boats from Tiberias landed near the place where the people had eaten the bread after the Lord had given thanks. Once the crowd realized that neither Jesus nor his disciples were there, they got into the boats and went to Capernaum in search of Jesus. When they found him on the other side of the lake, they asked him, "Rabbi, when did you get here?"*

*Jesus answered, "Very truly I tell you, you are looking for me, not because you saw the signs I performed but because you ate the loaves and had your fill. Do not work for food that spoils, but for food that endures to eternal life, which the Son of Man will give you. For on him God the Father has placed his seal of approval." Then they asked him, "What must we do to do the works God requires?" Jesus answered, "The work of God is this: to believe in the one he has sent." So they asked him, "What sign then will you give that we may see it and believe you? What will you do?*

# Jesus: Understanding the Mission

In Richmond, VA there is a building products business that has been around since the 1940's. The management attributes their success to having a vision that everyone in the company knows and puts into practice. As a matter of fact, employees are often pulled aside and asked to recite the mission statement verbatim. They do this so that the values of the company are integrated into every task and with every customer contact.

Jesus also knew the purpose of his mission when he walked this earth. He clearly spoke about the kingdom of God, faith, salvation, and the state of each human soul, but he constantly had to correct misunderstandings that seemed to crop up all around him. In John's Gospel, over 10,000 people had just been miraculously fed a meal of fish and bread. What an awesome experience! Life-changing, right? Not in the way one would think, as we will see.

I wonder if Jesus anticipated their response or, in his humanity was he genuinely surprised? Immediately after the sit-down dinner, Jesus withdrew by himself and the disciples started sailing across the sea toward Capernaum where they probably hoped for some rest and relief from the crowds. During the night a storm rose up and the disciples' boat was in danger of capsizing. Jesus, as master of all creation, came walking across the water to them. Why not? If he could bring people back from the dead, heal diseases and multiply loaves and fishes, was anything too hard?

The crowds, having been wowed by the feast the day before, wanted to find Jesus again. So they hired some boats and they, too, crossed the sea to find Jesus and the disciples. But they had remembered that Jesus didn't go with the disciples in the boat. Hey, how'd you get here? Jesus' response: *"I say to you, you seek me, not because you saw the signs, but because you ate of the loaves and were filled."* Jesus did not trust their motivation.

After the meal some of the men professed, *"This is truly the Prophet who is to come into the world."* Several hours later, when they were with Jesus in this moment, I think they were honestly trying to figure him out. Having been influenced by the instruction of their religious teachers, they had forgotten God's original company policy of grace and mercy and they made the same mistake as the rich young man (who wanted to know which commandments were best to obey) and the woman at the well (who was tired of drawing water from a well). They asked him, *"What shall we do, that we may work the works of God?"*

This question revealed their ignorance because one who was literate in biblical teaching would have known that it is only by God's grace that anyone is saved. Earlier Jesus had asked Nicodemus, *"Are you the teacher of Israel, and you do not know these things?" "You must be born again."* In other words, you need a new nature, a transformed heart, and a changed mind. Nothing you do will ever appease a righteous and holy God.

So, they had asked the wrong question. But Jesus in his infinite patience responds, *"This is the work of God, that you believe in Him whom He sent."* Well, that wasn't very satisfying, so they came up with bad question #2: *"What other sign will you perform then, that we may see it and believe you?"*

At this time in history, the teachings of Aristotle would have been prevalent in their education. Had they missed class that day? In developing a logical argument, one asks three questions: 1) Is it reasonable? 2) Does it relate to me? 3) Is the person speaking credible? Jesus had demonstrated sufficient answers to all these questions and yet they still had not put all the pieces together.

In many homes at Christmas you'll see the word "Believe" in wooden letters on the mantle or on a book shelf. Of course, that's all about Santa isn't it? And the belief is simply the will to have positive thoughts about a rotund man with a white beard who has flying reindeer and squeezes down millions of chimneys to bring presents. That indeed does take some concentration to imagine all that as real. So, what was Jesus saying when he said, *"believe in the one whom he sent."* Fortunately, we have the whole Bible to tell us about him. We have historical and personal accounts and sound theology, which leads us to make a solid decision about what we believe.

Belief in Jesus as Lord and Savior is not unlike adhering to our company's mission statement. We accept it and we put it into action by acting on its principles. You don't create or make an addendum to your company's statement, it is merely your responsibility to follow it and support it. And when Jesus tells us to "believe", he is reminding the people that salvation has always been about God's grace and mercy to save us. Do not add nor take away from what he has said is so.

Application:
1) Every business has a mission. In your experience, how has management enforced or encouraged adherence to its company principles?
2) Do your superiors appreciate creativity and imagination when it comes to following the mission or do they simply want adherence?
3) How can logic lead you to make better decisions?
4) How might you paraphrase Jesus' statement, *"Believe in the one he has sent."*
5) What one thing can you do today to help your company be successful or if unemployed, what one thing do you have to offer that will help solve a company's problems?

*I warn everyone who hears the words of the prophecy of this scroll: If anyone adds anything to them, God will add to that person the plagues described in this scroll. And if anyone takes words away from this scroll of prophecy, God will take away from that person any share in the tree of life and in the Holy City, which are described in this scroll. He who testifies to these things says, "Yes, I am coming soon." Amen. Come, Lord Jesus.*
(Revelation 22:18-20)

# Day 30

We Begin with God's Word

John 6:25-59

[Verses 25-30 are repeated from the day before in order to remind the reader of the context]
*When they found him on the other side of the lake, they asked him, "Rabbi, when did you get here?" Jesus answered, "Very truly I tell you, you are looking for me, not because you saw the signs I performed but because you ate the loaves and had your fill. Do not work for food that spoils, but for food that endures to eternal life, which the Son of Man will give you. For on him God the Father has placed his seal of approval." Then they asked him, "What must we do to do the works God requires?" Jesus answered, "The work of God is this: to believe in the one he has sent." So they asked him, "What sign then will you give that we may see it and believe you? What will you do? Our ancestors ate the manna in the wilderness; as it is written: 'He gave them bread from heaven to eat.'"*

*Jesus said to them, "Very truly I tell you, it is not Moses who has given you the bread from heaven, but it is my Father who gives you the true bread from heaven. For the bread of God is the bread that comes down from heaven and gives life to the world." "Sir," they said, "always give us this bread."*

*Then Jesus declared, "I am the bread of life. Whoever comes to me will never go hungry, and whoever believes in me will never be thirsty. But as I told you, you have seen me and still you do not believe. All those the Father gives me will come to me, and whoever comes to me I will never drive away. For I have come down from heaven not to do my will but to do the will of him who sent me. And this is the will of him who sent me, that I shall lose none of all those he has given me, but raise them up at the last day. For my Father's will is that everyone who looks to the Son and believes in him shall have eternal life, and I will raise them up at the last day."*

*At this the Jews there began to grumble about him because he said, "I am the bread that came down from heaven." They said, "Is this not Jesus, the son of Joseph, whose father and mother we know? How can he now say, 'I came down from heaven'?" "Stop grumbling among yourselves," Jesus answered. "No one can come to me unless the Father who sent me draws them, and I will raise them up at the last day. It is written in the Prophets: 'They will all be taught by God.' Everyone who has heard the Father and learned from him comes to me. No one has seen the Father except the one who is from God; only he has seen the Father. Very truly I tell you, the one who believes has eternal life.*

*I am the bread of life. Your ancestors ate the manna in the wilderness, yet they died. But here is the bread that comes down from heaven, which anyone may eat and not die. I am the living bread that came down from heaven. Whoever eats this bread will live forever. This bread is my flesh, which I will give for the life of the world." Then the Jews began to argue sharply among themselves, "How can this man give us his flesh to eat?" Jesus said to them, "Very truly I tell you, unless you eat the flesh of the Son of Man and drink his blood, you have no life in you. Whoever eats my flesh and drinks my blood has eternal life, and I will raise them up at the last day. For my flesh is real food and my blood is real drink. Whoever eats my flesh and drinks my blood remains in me, and I in them. Just as the living Father sent me and I live because of the Father, so the one who feeds on me will live because of me. This is the bread that came down from heaven. Your ancestors ate manna and died, but whoever feeds on this bread will live forever." He said this while teaching in the synagogue in Capernaum.*

# Jesus: Fulfillment of the Contract - Part 1

How many times have updates come across your screen and you scrolled through the morass of fine print to get to the button at the bottom where you click:

**I AGREE**

How trusting we are? Many of us would say we are skeptical of authority, distrusting of the political machine, wary of smooth-talking salesmen, and yet we will not take the time to read contracts which may involve personal privacy, invasion into personal finances or a threat to our cyber security.

What if the contract we signed either for our home or employment, put the onus on the bank or employer? What I mean is this, if the home did not meet to your satisfaction after 3 months, the bank would refund your money. Or if the job you moved across the country for didn't measure up to your expectation, your employer would either work overtime to make it up to you or find you another job. Unheard of, right?

In the today's passage, Jesus described a reality that the Jewish people should have understood. Their forefathers had "signed a contract" with Abraham 2000 years before but they had filed away the fine print and forgotten the true identity of the God they worshiped. God had promised that if He ever reneged on His promises, He himself, would cease to exist.

So Jesus, coming as God incarnate, reminds them that Moses did not give them the manna, but God. If they could accept this then couldn't they have accepted that Jesus, the Son of God, was the true bread from heaven? As the Messiah, the promised one, the one who just fed them physical bread, the one who walked on water, the one who healed the sick, had now, in bold print, revealed that his body was real food and his blood was real drink.

But they couldn't make the leap. This seemed too crazy. *"Is this not Jesus, the son of Joseph, whose father and mother we know?"* Even Jesus' appearance was a fulfillment of prophecy. The prophet Isaiah said, *"He had no beauty or majesty to attract us to him, nothing in his appearance that we should desire him."* The claims of Jesus seemed too extraordinary.

But were they? If we would take time to read the fine print we would recognize that Jesus did not come to this earth in an ill-timed, unexpected way. From Genesis to Malachi, God's plan for our salvation was foretold in great detail. But as we learn in this passage, spiritual things are spiritually discerned. The literal (or literary) meaning of Jesus' words remind us that the words were written in context. When Jesus said my flesh and blood are real food, the people should have known that his words had another meaning. *"This bread is my flesh, which I will give for the life of the world."* Language that we now understand referred to his crucifixion.

Nicodemus was told that *"he must be born again."* Spiritual language for radical change. In John 15 Jesus is seen as the *"true vine" and* we must be grafted into him. In John 10 Jesus said, *"I am the gate for the sheep."* He was also said to be the good Shepherd that watches over us. In plain language and in context we can understand the terms of the contract without reading more than what is there or less than what is intended.

The fine print in our lives can make all the difference, as well as the context. In my job do I understand the commitment I made to support the company's mission? In relationships, *"do to others what you would have them do to you."* In my faith, do I grasp the all-inclusive nature of a commitment to Christ? The radical nature of following Jesus Christ is offensive to a mindset settled in a worldview that is grounded only in earth-bound thinking. But if we can pray for spiritual discernment and see life from God's perspective, (the one he gives us in Scripture), then there is hope that we will find contentment and purpose.

Application:
1) Describe a time when not reading the fine print got you in trouble.
2) Have you ever entered into a contract (job, housing, relationship) where the other person went above and beyond the written rules to make sure you were satisfied?
3) Have you, like the Jewish people in Jesus' day, missed the point of Jesus' message by reading your own meaning into Scripture or not hearing as it was intended? How would you know?
4) What difference will absorbing the truth of this passage make in how you face today?

\*   \*   \*

*"I am the good shepherd. The good shepherd lays down his life for the sheep."*
(John 10:11)

# Day 31

We Begin with God's Word

John 6:60-71

*On hearing it ("Very truly I tell you, unless you eat the flesh of the Son of Man and drink his blood, you have no life in you.), many of his disciples said, "This is a hard teaching. Who can accept it?" Aware that his disciples were grumbling about this, Jesus said to them, "Does this offend you? Then what if you see the Son of Man ascend to where he was before! The Spirit gives life; the flesh counts for nothing. The words I have spoken to you—they are full of the Spirit and life. Yet there are some of you who do not believe." For Jesus had known from the beginning which of them did not believe and who would betray him. He went on to say, "This is why I told you that no one can come to me unless the Father has enabled them."*

*From this time many of his disciples turned back and no longer followed him. "You do not want to leave too, do you?" Jesus asked the Twelve. Simon Peter answered him, "Lord, to whom shall we go? You have the words of eternal life. We have come to believe and to know that you are the Holy One of God." Then Jesus replied, "Have I not chosen you, the Twelve? Yet one of you is a devil!" (He meant Judas, the son of Simon Iscariot, who, though one of the Twelve, was later to betray him.)*

# Jesus: Fulfillment of the Contract Part 2

What happens when you start a job with visions of your importance and the opportunity to make a difference and then you discover that you are just another cog in a big machine? I've had friends, after two weeks on a new job, come face to face with the reality that there is no perfect job. Humans are often optimistic and frequently idealistic, and the realistic assessment of ourselves and others can be startling without a firm grasp of the nature of this world and the hope that's held out to us.

If we had been with Jesus while he was on this earth and paid attention to what he said, then we might have grasped the hope that only he could offer. The hope of eternal life. Up to this point in the passage, Jesus had demonstrated his power over nature by walking on water, performed multiple miracles and spoken some strange words about his body being real food and his blood being real drink. Some were confused because they were so earth-bound. They did not understand Jesus' words as being spiritual and they certainly could not anticipate his eventual death and resurrection which would have clarified much.

This reminds me of Jesus' conversation with the disciples in reference to the 'yeast of the Pharisees when he said, *"How is it you don't understand that I was not talking to you about bread?"* (Matthew 16:11) And *"I have spoken to you of earthly things and you do not believe; how then will you believe if I speak of heavenly things?"* (John 3:12)

Many people were following Jesus because he did cool things. He challenged the Pharisees, who kept the people in a legalistic bind. He healed the sick and cast out demons. He provided a miraculous meal of bread and fish to thousands. And his words themselves were compelling. The Gospel writer Luke said, *"They were amazed at his teaching, because his words had authority."* (Luke 4:32)

Jesus asked, *"Does this offend you?"* The Apostle Paul reflected on Jesus' claims and remarks in 2 Corinthians 2:16, *"To the one we are an aroma that brings death; to the other, an aroma that brings life."* It should be no surprise that John recorded, *"From this time many of his disciples turned back and no longer followed him."* Maybe you had an experience working for a boss who pushed the envelope a bit too far or the new company policy was a bit over reaching. One response can be compared to those who left Jesus, *"This is a hard teaching. Who can accept it?"* Another could be like that of the disciples, *"Lord, to whom shall we go? You have the words of eternal life."*

In other words, we don't quite get it, but we trust you. We'll hold on a little longer hoping that even these hard words will make sense some day. I'm learning a lot in my present job. Some things I get right away, others, I'll need practice and further explanation. If I quit the first time I have a disagreement or misunderstanding I won't last long anywhere. Judas reminds me of people who come into a group or organization with preconceived ideas, obtuse opinions and poor logic. His mind was bent toward self-interest and twisted reasoning. So much so that Jesus called him a devil. Know anyone like that?

So, how will we approach today knowing that we do not have complete knowledge of our situations or the people around us? We often enter employment the same way we enter into faith. It all begins with trust.

Application:
1. When have you entered a job with certain expectations only to learn very quickly that things are not what they seemed in the beginning?
2. What do you think it means to appropriately think about things as spiritual and earthly? What mistakes did the people in Jesus' day make and what mistakes do we make today?
3. Have you ever given up on a job or a person too quickly? Perhaps your judgment was premature or you ran into an anomaly that would have been unusual for anyone.
4. How can we maintain healthy skepticism and still give others the benefit of the doubt?
5. Peter speaks for the rest of the 12 disciples, *"Lord, to whom shall we go? You have the words of eternal life. We have come to believe and to know that you are the Holy One of God."* Neutrality is impossible. Does Peter speak for you? Explain.

\*     \*     \*

*For we are to God the pleasing aroma of Christ among those who are being saved and those who are perishing. To the one we are an aroma that brings death; to the other, an aroma that brings life. And who is equal to such a task?*
(2 Corinthians 2:14-16)

# Day 32

We Begin with God's Word

John 8:2-11

*At dawn he [Jesus] appeared again in the temple courts, where all the people gathered around him, and he sat down to teach them. The teachers of the law and the Pharisees brought in a woman caught in adultery. They made her stand before the group and said to Jesus, "Teacher, this woman was caught in the act of adultery. In the Law Moses commanded us to stone such women. Now what do you say?" They were using this question as a trap, in order to have a basis for accusing him.*

*But Jesus bent down and started to write on the ground with his finger. When they kept on questioning him, he straightened up and said to them, "Let any one of you who is without sin be the first to throw a stone at her." Again he stooped down and wrote on the ground.*

*At this, those who heard began to go away one at a time, the older ones first, until only Jesus was left, with the woman still standing there. Jesus straightened up and asked her, "Woman, where are they? Has no one condemned you?" "No one, sir," she said. "Then neither do I condemn you," Jesus declared. "Go now and leave your life of sin."*

## Jesus: True Bearing

One of the most impressive characteristics of Jesus was his bearing. He had the ability to remain composed and self-assured in the most difficult situations. Up to this point in John's Gospel, Jesus had made some audacious claims. There was no mystery here. He said in language that his hearers could understand that he was the long-awaited Messiah. But it was difficult for the people to comprehend because the Scriptures had been distorted by their teachers and their socio-political situation was so dire that they had formulated their own image of what a Messiah should look like.

Those of us who have been unemployed know what it's like to view the world with jaded eyes. Rejection after rejection can cause one to have a fairly pessimistic point of view. How did Jesus maintain his disposition in the midst of death threats and unbelief? And how can we develop a bearing that is confident, courageous and all-together positive without overstating ourselves by slipping into a fantasy that over estimates our talents and abilities?

In this passage the Pharisees pull out all the stops in order to corner Jesus. *"They brought a woman caught in adultery"*. Their very basis for this case began in a flawed manner; one person cannot commit adultery; it takes two to tango, so to speak. They proceeded to misquote the Scriptures by saying a woman caught in adultery ought to be stoned according to the Law of Moses. The Law actually says, according to Leviticus 20:10 that both people were to be put to death, but stoning was not specified.

Jesus shows he is more honorable by his response. He squats down and writes in the dirt. But that doesn't deter the Pharisees, *"they kept on questioning him"*. If you've ever been in an interview where the questions come rapid-fire, you will know what this feels like. You can't answer fast enough and you can't give sufficient answers before the next question comes. This is where we often coach people to *'take control of the interview'*. Don't let an HR person badger you or proceed with an agenda that isn't helpful. Derail their questioning by telling a story or respectfully hijack the process by asking your own questions. In other words, maintain your bearing by being confident and courageous.

We don't know what Jesus was writing in the dirt, but some suggest that he, in his omniscience, was writing the sins of all the people standing there with rocks in their hands... *Sarah-gossip, Jeremiah-lying, Demetrius-cheating, Samuel-theft, Mary-lust* and so on. But Jesus remained silent. The Pharisees jabbered on with their accusations and the woman, who may have been stark naked in order to humiliate her and embarrass Jesus, was standing there, guilty, ashamed and ready to be condemned.

It is then that in Jesus' perfect timing, stood up and I like to imagine, looked each accuser in the eye and said, *"Let any one of you who is without sin be the first to throw a stone at her."* Wait a minute! Where is that in the Law? We're people of the Book. Quote a proverb or interpret Moses, but this? Jesus presents the great equalizer which the Apostle Paul later affirms in Romans 3:23 *"All have sinned and fallen short of the glory of God."*

The culture of that day had great respect for their elders, and it is they who dropped their stones first. They got it. Conviction gripped their souls and they couldn't escape the truth of Jesus' words. It would be like that one interview you had where you were asked what you knew to be a highly significant question and you nailed it with a story that you had prepared for just that moment. But Jesus didn't give a fist pump or high five his disciples, he simply squatted back down and began to write in the dirt again. Maybe this time he was crossing out the sins he had listed because that was why he came in the first place. John the Baptist had proclaimed. *"Look, the lamb of God who takes away the sin of the world!"*

A moment later he stood up and faced the woman. And I believe he looked her in the eyes with love and piercing concern and said, *"Woman, where are they? Has no one condemned you?"* The woman, weak from the ordeal, barely able to speak, says, *"No one, sir."* Now, Jesus as God and judge of the universe is uniquely qualified to condemn this woman. She had sinned. She had, according to God's own law, done something deserving of death. And the one person who can rightfully remove her from planet earth is standing in front of her. Why doesn't he? Because in this one story he demonstrates the reason he came. John had recorded him saying, *"I have come that they may have life, and have it to the full."* And also in John 3:17 *"For God did not send his Son into the world to condemn the world, but to save the world through him."*

The woman must have experienced a range of emotions: from fear to joy, confusion to relief. Alone with Jesus, he said two significant things: I'm not going to do what the law requires (because I am going to take the punishment upon myself) and stop sinning and receive this gift of life I am giving you. Jesus knew that, if the sin doesn't get her killed by those who are zealous for the Law, it will eat her from the inside out.

What an incredible message of freedom. No condemnation but a prescription for true living. You should never take a job where the manager is one who shames and blames or is an abuser, like the Pharisees in Jesus' day. A life in Christ frees us to live as we really should and enables us to walk with a bearing that communicates true courage and confidence.

Application:
1. Have you ever experienced an interview where you were able to take the lead or you wish you had?
2. Why do we judge others so quickly and so easily condemn?
3. Have you ever been forgiven when you didn't expect it?
4. Do you struggle to forgive?
5. Is there anything preventing you from experiencing the freedom that Jesus gave this woman?

*   *   *

*Let the wicked forsake their ways and the unrighteous their thoughts. Let them turn to the Lord, and he will have mercy on them, and to our God, for he will freely pardon.*
(Isaiah 55:7 )

# Day 33

We Begin with God's Word

1 Samuel 1:1-17

*There was a certain man from Ramathaim, a Zuphite from the hill country of Ephraim, whose name was Elkanah son of Jeroham, the son of Elihu, the son of Tohu, the son of Zuph, an Ephraimite. He had two wives; one was called Hannah and the other Peninnah. Peninnah had children, but Hannah had none.*

*Year after year this man went up from his town to worship and sacrifice to the Lord Almighty at Shiloh, where Hophni and Phinehas, the two sons of Eli, were priests of the Lord. Whenever the day came for Elkanah to sacrifice, he would give portions of the meat to his wife Peninnah and to all her sons and daughters. But to Hannah he gave a double portion because he loved her, and the Lord had closed her womb. Because the Lord had closed Hannah's womb, her rival kept provoking her in order to irritate her. This went on year after year. Whenever Hannah went up to the house of the Lord, her rival provoked her till she wept and would not eat. Her husband Elkanah would say to her, "Hannah, why are you weeping? Why don't you eat? Why are you downhearted? Don't I mean more to you than ten sons?"*

*Once when they had finished eating and drinking in Shiloh, Hannah stood up. Now Eli the priest was sitting on his chair by the doorpost of the Lord's house. In her deep anguish Hannah prayed to the Lord, weeping bitterly. And she made a vow, saying, "Lord Almighty, if you will only look on your servant's misery and remember me, and not forget your servant but give her a son, then I will give him to the Lord for all the days of his life, and no razor will ever be used on his head."*

*As she kept on praying to the Lord, Eli observed her mouth. Hannah was praying in her heart, and her lips were moving but her voice was not heard. Eli thought she was drunk and said to her, "How long are you going to stay drunk? Put away your wine." "Not so, my lord," Hannah replied, "I am a woman who is deeply troubled. I have not been drinking wine or beer; I was pouring out my soul to the Lord. Do not take your servant for a wicked woman; I have been praying here out of my great anguish and grief." Eli answered, "Go in peace, and may the God of Israel grant you what you have asked of him."*

# Hannah:
# A Righteous Woman in Sinful Times

It seemed like a good idea at the time. The place was right. My wife was happy. All seemed to be lining up. Only in hindsight can I now see my mistakes and the mistakes of the company that hired me. In the final interview it became clear that the CEO had views contrary to mine and yet I imagined that these could be overcome. I ignored the red flags that were waving violently in the wind. From the perspective of the company, they had been operating at a deficit for years and should never have hired me. Of course, I didn't find this out until we were two years in.

So, after 2 1/2 years I had to leave due to financial reasons. Others outside of the company but familiar with the situation told me that my ideological conflicts would have eventually forced me to leave anyway. I started wondering, *"Why is this happening to me? Did I do something to bring about this problem? Is it someone else's fault?" Good questions to ask, but be ready to own up to the answers.*

In the today's passage, we find a situation where several societal and organizational problems contributed to one person's misery. Elkanah, an otherwise upstanding member of his community, had married two women. Something prohibited since the beginning of time. God had instituted marriage between one man and one woman. Commentators suspect that because Hannah could not bear children, Elkanah had married Peninnah who then, obviously, became a rival to Hannah, his first wife.

Why was Hannah barren? Certainly it was the result of living in a fallen world but as we go on in the story we discover that God had plans for her, just as he had plans for Sarah and Rebekah, other Old Testament matriarchs who had experienced God's miraculous healing powers.

In regards to the characters of the two women, you would think that Peninnah's fertile womb would have made her a joyful and delightful person, but she handled her blessing with arrogance and disdain. While Hannah, who felt cursed, was loved more by her husband and humbly prayed to God for relief from her lifelong malady. Blessings and curses are all a test aren't they? How we handle them reveals our character and integrity.

Hannah demonstrated her character when she was found by the priest, Eli, praying in the temple. This temple which had been abused by Eli's sons, may have had many women of ill repute loitering on its premises. So, when Eli saw her mouthing words but making no sound, he figured she was one of them and accused her of being drunk. Her response was one of respect and humility: *"Not so, my lord....Do not take your servant for a wicked woman; I have been praying here out of my great anguish and grief."*

Her response to Eli brings about a blessing from God. *"Go in peace, and may the God of Israel grant you what you have asked of him."* It's not wrong to defend yourself when wrongly accused, but our approach can make all the difference. Hannah surely knew the stories of her ancestors and believed in a God who was sovereign. Her prayer was honest, heartfelt, and trusting.

In this instance God answered her prayer by giving her a son, a son she had dedicated to God. When he was old enough she gave him to Eli to continue to raise in the temple. Hannah's song of praise in chapter 2 was to the Gift Giver and not to the gift of a son. Today, we are often guilty of focusing on the thing, whether it be obtaining a job, buying a car or getting an education, and we forget the One that makes it all possible.

Hannah's song in chapter 2 begins, *"My heart rejoices in the Lord." "There is no one holy like the Lord." "The Lord brings death and makes alive."* These thematic refrains make it obvious that Hannah, unlike Peninnah who bragged about her ability to have children, was focused on the One who can give life and can take it away.

One commentator stated, *"Are we poor? God made us poor, which is a good reason why we should be content, and reconcile ourselves to our condition. Are we rich? God made us rich, which is a good reason why we should be thankful, and serve him cheerfully in the abundance of good things he gives us."* [Matthew Henry]

Can Hannah's story help us today as we struggle to gain perspective in the midst of the trials we are experiencing? Can we thank God whether we are poor or rich? Can we trust that the God of the universe is not only in complete control but he is also good?

I have made a lot more mistakes since being let go from that one company. And I've been subjected to other's bad decisions and I still live in a world that, though often beautiful, is fraught with problems. I am trying to see life from Hannah's point of view, *"My heart rejoices in the Lord; in the Lord my horn is lifted high."*

Application:
1. Are you living with regret over a mistake you made years ago rather than trusting that God can bring good even out of the worst circumstances?
2. Are you willing to admit your mistakes, seek forgiveness? Are you willing to forgive other's mistakes?
3. What would it look like for you to focus on the Giver rather than the gift?
4. What difference does God's sovereignty make? Does it bring comfort or fear?

\* \* \*

*"For the foundations of the earth are the Lord's; on them he has set the world. He will guard the feet of his faithful servants, but the wicked will be silenced in the place of darkness."*
(1 Samuel 2:8b-9)

# Day 34

We Begin with God's Word

1 Samuel 2:12-36

*Eli's sons were scoundrels; they had no regard for the Lord. Now it was the practice of the priests that, whenever any of the people offered a sacrifice, the priest's servant would come with a three-pronged fork in his hand while the meat was being boiled and would plunge the fork into the pan or kettle or caldron or pot. Whatever the fork brought up the priest would take for himself. This is how they treated all the Israelites who came to Shiloh. But even before the fat was burned, the priest's servant would come and say to the person who was sacrificing, "Give the priest some meat to roast; he won't accept boiled meat from you, but only raw." If the person said to him, "Let the fat be burned first, and then take whatever you want," the servant would answer, "No, hand it over now; if you don't, I'll take it by force." This sin of the young men was very great in the Lord's sight, for they were treating the Lord's offering with contempt.*

*But Samuel was ministering before the Lord—a boy wearing a linen ephod. Each year his mother made him a little robe and took it to him when she went up with her husband to offer the annual sacrifice. Eli would bless Elkanah and his wife, saying, "May the Lord give you children by this woman to take the place of the one she prayed for and gave to the Lord." Then they would go home. And the Lord was gracious to Hannah; she gave birth to three sons and two daughters. Meanwhile, the boy Samuel grew up in the presence of the Lord.*

*Now Eli, who was very old, heard about everything his sons were doing to all Israel and how they slept with the women who served at the entrance to the tent of meeting. So he said to them, "Why do you do such things? I hear from all the people about these wicked deeds of yours. No, my sons; the report I hear spreading among the Lord's people is not good. If one person sins against another, God may mediate for the offender; but if anyone sins against the Lord, who will intercede for them?" His sons, however, did not listen to their father's rebuke, for it was the Lord's will to put them to death.*

*And the boy Samuel continued to grow in stature and in favor with the Lord and with people. Now a man of God came to Eli and said to him, "This is what the Lord says: 'Did I not clearly reveal myself to your ancestor's family when they were in Egypt under Pharaoh? I chose your ancestor out of all the tribes of Israel to be my priest, to go up to my altar, to burn incense, and to wear an ephod in my presence. I also gave your ancestor's family all the food offerings presented by the Israelites. Why do you scorn my sacrifice and offering that I prescribed for my dwelling? Why do you honor your sons more than me by fattening yourselves on the choice parts of every offering made by my people Israel?'*

*"Therefore the Lord, the God of Israel, declares: 'I promised that members of your family would minister before me forever.' But now the Lord declares: 'Far be it from me! Those who honor me I will honor, but those who despise me will be disdained. The time is coming when I will cut short your strength and the strength of your priestly house, so that no one in it will reach old age, and you will see distress in my dwelling. Although good will be done to Israel, no one in your family line*

will ever reach old age. Every one of you that I do not cut off from serving at my altar I will spare only to destroy your sight and sap your strength, and all your descendants will die in the prime of life.

"'And what happens to your two sons, Hophni and Phinehas, will be a sign to you—they will both die on the same day. I will raise up for myself a faithful priest, who will do according to what is in my heart and mind. I will firmly establish his priestly house, and they will minister before my anointed one always. Then everyone left in your family line will come and bow down before him for a piece of silver and a loaf of bread and plead, "Appoint me to some priestly office so I can have food to eat."'"

# My Employer is a Son of the Devil

The best definition of integrity is: *"Who am I when no one is looking?"* In one of my first jobs out of college I worked in a retail lumber store as the Night Manager. When the General Manager had a day off, the Assistant Manager would be in charge, and his behavior was radically different when the boss wasn't around. He sat in his office much of the day and did little to move the company forward. It was difficult for me to stay motivated, and I felt little compulsion to say anything to make things right. Our passage describes a time in ancient history when the cast of characters is different but the human predicament is familiar.

The context of 1 Samuel 2 was a time when there was no king. Israel was a theocracy and the center of Israel's worship and government was the temple. Eli was the priest and his sons, Hophni and Phineas worked under him as assistants. With Eli aging the sons gained more and more authority and despite Eli's pleading they did more and more evil. Verse 12 says, *"Eli's sons were scoundrels;"* the word scoundrel can be translated as wicked, despicable, evil, good for nothing, corrupt, worthless and the most descriptive - sons of the devil.

The Law of God as given through Moses was very prescriptive as to how to make an offering to the Lord. From the offerings, excess meat was to feed the priests who neither owned land nor made a living in any other way. But Hophni and Phineas didn't think it was enough to get the leftovers. They wanted the best of the sacrifice which God had required for himself, thus desecrating the altar. They also had adulterous relationships with the women who served in the temple. The worst of it was that they not only sinned, but made the nation Israel sin as well by leading them astray in worship.

Eli heard of these things and he scolded his sons, but he never disciplined them in a way that made them stop. One commentator states, "It is sometimes necessary that we put an edge upon the reproofs we give. There are those that must be saved with fear."[Matthew Henry] In other words, unless we know that we have something to lose we will never change our behavior. The assistant manager at my store was able to hide his behavior from the manager as long as the other employees, including myself, didn't turn him in. Because of his character defect he had no incentive to change on his own.

Young Samuel begins his service in the temple in the midst of these corrupt times. He didn't know anything about serving in the temple but he could light a candle, or hold a dish, or run on an errand, or shut a door. He begins well by being willing to do the slightest task in order to serve. Entering a new job can be intimidating and it's obvious that we will not know everything at once, but let us do what we know how to do in order to justify our hiring.

Those that have been with a company for a long period of time may come to feel entitled. Hophni and Phineas probably did not begin their misbehavior all at once. A little bit at a time they slipped away from the standards of the temple. So subtly that the people of Israel did not object because they were ignorant of the Law. They depended upon the priests to instruct them.

A time of reformation was at hand and in order for that to happen, a house cleaning was required. *"His sons, however, did not listen to their father's rebuke, for it was the Lord's will to put them to death."* Eli had the power and authority to change the destiny of his sons. His sons could have repented and changed the fate of the future of their families. Their repeated evil and abuse of power hardened their hearts to such an extent that repentance became impossible.

The prophet of the Lord came to Eli and told him, *"I will raise up for myself a faithful priest, who will do according to what is in my heart and mind. I will firmly establish his priestly house, and they will minister before my anointed one always."* But Eli's family line will not continue because of the egregious sins of his family. *"The time is coming when I will cut short your strength and the strength of your priestly house, so that no one in it will reach old age."*

The assistant manager, like Hophni and Phineas may have gotten away with their behavior for a time, but nothing escapes the watchful eyes of God. Who are you trying to please today? What secrets are you hiding? Yours? Others? If we serve as an accomplice to another's sin, we are just as guilty. I wish I had had the courage to speak to that Assistant Manager, but I hope I have tried to make amends over the years by doing my job, no matter how menial at times, with strength and integrity.

Application:
1) When was a time that you covered up for someone who was slacking off?
2) Has someone ever covered for you?
3) If you have had someone confront you about your work ethic, how did you respond?
4) How can you be like Samuel, willing to do whatever it takes to get the job done?

5) What can you do in your situation today to expose deceit, encourage hard work and pursue integrity?

        \*     \*     \*

*"Those who honor me I will honor, but those who despise me will be disdained."*
(1 Samuel 2:30b)

# Day 35

We Begin with God's Word

1 Samuel 3:1-20

*The boy Samuel ministered before the Lord under Eli. In those days the word of the Lord was rare; there were not many visions. One night Eli, whose eyes were becoming so weak that he could barely see, was lying down in his usual place. The lamp of God had not yet gone out, and Samuel was lying down in the house of the Lord, where the ark of God was. Then the Lord called Samuel. Samuel answered, "Here I am." And he ran to Eli and said, "Here I am; you called me." But Eli said, "I did not call; go back and lie down." So he went and lay down.*

*Again the Lord called, "Samuel!" And Samuel got up and went to Eli and said, "Here I am; you called me." "My son," Eli said, "I did not call; go back and lie down." Now Samuel did not yet know the Lord: The word of the Lord had not yet been revealed to him. A third time the Lord called, "Samuel!" And Samuel got up and went to Eli and said, "Here I am; you called me." Then Eli realized that the Lord was calling the boy. So Eli told Samuel, "Go and lie down, and if he calls you, say, 'Speak, Lord, for your servant is listening.'" So Samuel went and lay down in his place.*

*The Lord came and stood there, calling as at the other times, "Samuel! Samuel!" Then Samuel said, "Speak, for your servant is listening." And the Lord said to Samuel: "See, I am about to do something in Israel that will make the ears of everyone who hears about it tingle. At that time I will carry out against Eli everything I spoke against his family—from beginning to end. For I told him that I would judge his family forever because of the sin he knew about; his sons blasphemed God, and he failed to restrain them. Therefore I swore to the house of Eli, 'The guilt of Eli's house will never be atoned for by sacrifice or offering.'"* Samuel lay down until morning and then opened the doors of the house of the Lord. He was afraid to tell Eli the vision, but Eli called him and said, "Samuel, my son." Samuel answered, "Here I am." "What was it he said to you?" Eli asked. "Do not hide it from me. May God deal with you, be it ever so severely, if you hide from me anything he told you." So Samuel told him everything, hiding nothing from him. Then Eli said, "He is the Lord; let him do what is good in his eyes."

The Lord was with Samuel as he grew up, and he let none of Samuel's words fall to the ground. And all Israel from Dan to Beersheba recognized that Samuel was attested as a prophet of the Lord.

# Waiting? Unemployed? The Time is Right

How long have you been waiting, unemployed or underemployed? How have you used your time in this interim period? In Career Prospectors we talk a lot about what we do with this new free time and offer all kinds of volunteer opportunities to teach social media classes, help set up the Career Expo, attend networking meetings and more. We want to be able to concretely answer that question about that gap in our unemployment.

I happen to be an expert in this field. Since I brought my family back from Cameroon in 2011, I have worked on a farm, in a mental health hospital, started my own business, volunteered at Career Prospectors, pastored a church, worked with an inner city ministry and also in the retail world. I am convinced that God has called me to be a pastor and throughout all these career moves I have striven to minister to people wherever I find myself.

The context of today's passage is a time when Israel was not being well-shepherded by the religious leaders. Eli, the priest, was neglectful, and his sons were abusive, thus both setting poor examples for the people. But God was on the move. In *The Chronicles of Narnia* by C.S. Lewis there was a time when Narnia was under a curse, so all was cold, frozen, and barren. As a thaw began, the creatures of the land could tell something was happening and they attributed it to the great Lion, Aslan. A rumor went throughout the land, *"Aslan is on the move."* The inhabitants of Narnia knew that this was significant and waited with great anticipation.

A commentator states, *"God will never leave himself without a witness nor his church without a guide."[Matthew Henry]* Maybe you have experienced your own time of wilderness or have wondered where God was as you went through a very difficult time. You are not alone. Biblical history reminds us that many times God seemed to withdraw His hand. Think of the four hundred years that Israel was in Egypt or the twenty five years that Abraham had to wait until Isaac was born. But was God ever absent? Absolutely not! Romans 5:6 states that, *"at just the right time, when we were still powerless, Christ died for the ungodly."*

The Bible reminds us that God's timing is perfect. When Lazarus was dying, Jesus chose to stay away. 2 Peter 3:8 reminds us not to *"forget this one thing, dear friends: 'With the Lord a day is like a thousand years, and a thousand years are like a day.'"* So, as Israel was floundering under Eli's leadership, God was actively working through Elkanah and Hannah as they produced a son. A son they named Samuel who would become a great prophet starting at a very early age.

1 Samuel 3:1 says, *"In those days the word of the Lord was rare; there were not many visions."* Out of the blue, God speaks to the boy Samuel and he is guided in hearing the Lord's voice by Eli. But what a terrible vision he receives. God entrusted to a small child the judgment on Eli's family. A vision that Samuel was not anxious to repeat. The Scriptures say, *"Samuel lay down until morning and then opened the doors of the house of the Lord."* He was afraid to tell Eli the vision.

A commentator states, *"God did not come to him now to tell him how great a man he should be in his day, what a figure he should make, and what a blessing he should be in Israel. Young people have commonly a great curiosity to be told their fortune, but God came to Samuel, not to gratify his curiosity, but to employ him in his service." [Matthew Henry]* Have we considered what God might be saying to us in our day?

Eli had a unique way of getting the information out of Samuel. *"Do not hide it from me. May God deal with you, be it ever so severely, if you hide from me anything he told you."* When Samuel tells Eli everything God had told him, Eli could have whimpered and complained but instead he said, *"He is the Lord; let him do what is good in his eyes."* Are we as willing to accept God's will? Do we believe that God is good so that anything that he allows will come to benefit me and the world around me even when the waiting seems unbearable, the disappointment excruciating, or the period of unemployment debilitating?

I have been using this season in my life to write these studies for my own and other's benefit . I have put it to the test in a weekly Bible study for those who are under-employed or unemployed. I meet with people in Career Prospectors who are asking hard questions about life. I also meet weekly with several men to study Scripture, hold each other accountable, and plan for the future. And I make known my handyman skills to take on occasional jobs. I know God has called me to be a pastor, and I am using the gifts he has given me to serve in anyway I can. I hope you will consider whatever resources God has given you and seek to be a servant wherever you find yourself.

Application:
1. How are you spending your time if you are in a period of waiting or unemployment? What else might you do to be productive?
2. When have you experienced a season of silence from God? What was that like for you?
3. How can you be listening intently for God's voice, ready to say, like Samuel, *"Speak Lord, for your servant is listening"?* In order to do this, you may need to "unplug" intentionally from all the noise of electronic devices at certain times of the day. This focus can allow you to listen for God and to God.
4. When you have experienced difficult times or times of discipline for mistakes or errors you have made, what has been your attitude? Can we say with Eli, *"It is the Lord, let him do what seemeth him good."* (Sometimes the King James sounds cool.)

Look forward to what God is going to do and imagine hearing this....

\* \* \*

*And the Lord said to Samuel: "See, I am about to do something in Israel that will make the ears of everyone who hears about it tingle.*
(1 Samuel 3:11)

# Day 36

We Begin with God's Word

Excerpts from 1 Samuel 8:1-10:1

*When Samuel grew old, he appointed his sons as Israel's leaders. The name of his firstborn was Joel and the name of his second was Abijah, and they served at Beersheba. But his sons did not follow his ways. They turned aside after dishonest gain and accepted bribes and perverted justice. So all the elders of Israel gathered together and came to Samuel at Ramah. They said to him, "You are old, and your sons do not follow your ways; now appoint a king to lead us, such as all the other nations have."*

*But when they said, "Give us a king to lead us," this displeased Samuel; so he prayed to the Lord. And the Lord told him: "Listen to all that the people are saying to you; it is not you they have rejected, but they have rejected me as their king. As they have done from the day I brought them up out of Egypt until this day, forsaking me and serving other gods, so they are doing to you. Now listen to them; but warn them solemnly and let them know what the king who will reign over them will claim as his rights."*

*…Now the day before Saul came, the Lord had revealed this to Samuel: "About this time tomorrow I will send you a man from the land of Benjamin. Anoint him ruler over my people Israel; he will deliver them from the hand of the Philistines. I have looked on my people, for their cry has reached me." When Samuel caught sight of Saul, the Lord said to him, "This is the man I spoke to you about; he will*

*govern my people."* Saul approached Samuel in the gateway and asked, *"Would you please tell me where the seer's house is?" "I am the seer,"* Samuel replied. *"Go up ahead of me to the high place, for today you are to eat with me, and in the morning I will send you on your way and will tell you all that is in your heart. As for the donkeys you lost three days ago, do not worry about them; they have been found. And to whom is all the desire of Israel turned, if not to you and your whole family line?"*

*Saul answered, "But am I not a Benjamite, from the smallest tribe of Israel, and is not my clan the least of all the clans of the tribe of Benjamin? Why do you say such a thing to me?" After they came down from the high place to the town, Samuel talked with Saul on the roof of his house. They rose about daybreak, and Samuel called to Saul on the roof, "Get ready, and I will send you on your way." When Saul got ready, he and Samuel went outside together. As they were going down to the edge of the town, Samuel said to Saul, "Tell the servant to go on ahead of us"—and the servant did so—"but you stay here for a while, so that I may give you a message from God." Then Samuel took a flask of olive oil and poured it on Saul's head and kissed him, saying, "Has not the Lord anointed you ruler over his inheritance?"*

# Be Careful What You Ask For

We often pray foolish and selfish prayers. We don't know any better. We think we know what we want and what we need, especially when we see others with the "ideal" job, house, car, spouse, children, etc. Envy and jealousy have no bounds. It's a good thing that we have a perfect, good and sovereign God who actually knows better than we do what is good for us.

To appreciate today's passage, let's recall the context. The nation of Israel at the time of Samuel was a theocracy. God was their king and he administered justice and rule through his prophets. The system was broken, however, because Eli's sons abused the people through the exploitation of the priesthood. They had a brief respite with Samuel for several years, but then even his sons misbehaved so much that it caused the people to wonder what it would be like to have consistent human leadership, like everyone else.

*"Give us a king"*. In this request they are not seeking Samuel's guidance, God's wisdom or accepting any of the blame for their misbehavior. One commentator observes, they demanded not, *"Give us a king that is wise and good, and will judge better than thy sons do," but, "Give us a king," anybody that will but make a figure."* [Matthew Henry] How many mistakes are made through impulsiveness or from lack of advice and wisdom? Israel had lost the vision that they were God's chosen people for the redemption of the world. Their history was one of God's intervention and miraculous activity but they had easily forgotten.

The pattern of Israel was to follow God when it was clear that they would be defeated or in a state of destitution without his help. They then would cry out to him. But when things were going well or they felt confident in their own strength, they relied on human ingenuity and wisdom. Are we any different? God tells Samuel, *"Listen to all that the people are saying to you; it is not you they have rejected, but they have rejected me as their king."* Before we judge them too harshly we should closely examine how we make decisions and what considerations we determine to be important.

Despite Samuel's warnings about how a king would treat them, they declare, *"We want a king over us. Then we will be like all the other nations, with a king to lead us and to go out before us and fight our battles."* Conformity to world standards brings a temporary peace and satisfaction because we hear the applause of the majority, but a hundred years later King Solomon wrote this, *"There is a way that appears to be right, but in the end it leads to death."*

God honors the people's request but uses the opportunity to discipline them as well. He gives them what they want, a king. Not just any king but *"as handsome a young man as could be found anywhere in Israel, and he was a head taller than anyone else."* Isn't this what they think will satisfy? As readers of history we should be skeptical about this choice. If we jump forward a few chapters, we can see what matters to people and what matters to God are often two different things. *"The Lord does not look at the things people look at. People look at the outward appearance, but the Lord looks at the heart"* (1 Samuel 16:7).

We cry out for God to answer our prayers. It's ironic that the only time I hear that God really did answer our prayers is when we get what we want. Things that seem to be good, like a job, deliverance from cancer, a baby, money, etc. But what if God delays? What if getting what we want is not good for us? What if when we pray, we pray for God's will rather than for our own selfish desires? What if being out of a job is better for us right now than being gainfully employed? Is it possible that, in God's wisdom, he has bigger plans for you and me than benefits and a paycheck?

Fortunately, God is not a cosmic gum ball machine into which we put our penny (quarter) and out comes exactly what we want. He is a good and gracious God who gives us what we need, and something we often don't consider: what will bring him the glory. Let's not be afraid to pray our pitiful, foolish or short-sighted prayers, but be ready for the best answer, *"one that you would not believe even if you were told"* (Habakkuk 1:5).

Application:
1. Can you identify with Eli and Samuel who did their best to raise their children only to have them rebel against your authority and values?
2. Likewise, have you done your best in your job, only to suffer the consequences of someone else's error or sin?
3. Have you experienced the benefits of suffering and the consequences of honor and wealth? *"Many that have done well in a state of meanness and subjection have been spoiled by preferment and power. Honours change men's minds, and too often for the worse."* [Matthew Henry]
4. Like the people in Samuel's day, have you ever jumped ahead of the good that God wants to do in order to get what you think you want?
5. Have you ever been pleasantly surprised by a circumstance or a person from which you would have never expected good? Describe the situation.

\*   \*   \*

*Do not be anxious about anything, but in every situation, by prayer and petition, with thanksgiving, present your requests to God. And the peace of God, which transcends all understanding, will guard your hearts and your minds in Christ Jesus.*
(Philippians 4:6,7)

# Day 37

We Begin with God's Word

1 Samuel 12:1-25

Samuel said to all Israel, "I have listened to everything you said to me and have set a king over you. Now you have a king as your leader. As for me, I am old and gray, and my sons are here with you. I have been your leader from my youth until this day. Here I stand. Testify against me in the presence of the Lord and his anointed. Whose ox have I taken? Whose donkey have I taken? Whom have I cheated? Whom have I oppressed? From whose hand have I accepted a bribe to make me shut my eyes? If I have done any of these things, I will make it right."  "You have not cheated or oppressed us," they replied. "You have not taken anything from anyone's hand."  Samuel said to them, "The Lord is witness against you, and also his anointed is witness this day, that you have not found anything in my hand."  "He is witness," they said.

"Now then, stand still and see this great thing the Lord is about to do before your eyes! Is it not wheat harvest now? I will call on the Lord to send thunder and rain. And you will realize what an evil thing you did in the eyes of the Lord when you asked for a king." Then Samuel called on the Lord, and that same day the Lord sent thunder and rain. So all the people stood in awe of the Lord and of Samuel.  The people all said to Samuel, "Pray to the Lord your God for your servants so that we will not die, for we have added to all our other sins the evil of asking for a king."

*"Do not be afraid," Samuel replied. "You have done all this evil; yet do not turn away from the Lord, but serve the Lord with all your heart. Do not turn away after useless idols. They can do you no good, nor can they rescue you, because they are useless. For the sake of his great name the Lord will not reject his people, because the Lord was pleased to make you his own. As for me, far be it from me that I should sin against the Lord by failing to pray for you. And I will teach you the way that is good and right. But be sure to fear the Lord and serve him faithfully with all your heart; consider what great things he has done for you. Yet if you persist in doing evil, both you and your king will perish."*

# Religion and Politics: Necessary Collaboration

Does religion affect what goes on in the market place? Does what I believe impact the way I behave toward my coworkers? Is it really a wise or intelligent thing to reveal my views on the nature of the universe and our purpose to my fellow employees? I would contend that these convictions either make us the best employee/boss or one that should be avoided at all costs.

Samuel, as God's prophet, was a priest but he was also the political leader of Israel. God worked through him to communicate laws that were for the ordering of society as well as temple worship. This was a Theocracy and was unique in the world at the time. The people, however, rejected God and demanded that Samuel appoint a purely political, human king, like the nations around them. The Israelites did not appreciate this privilege as a chosen people or anticipate the consequences of separating their religion from their politics.

Is the world any different today? What are the two things we are not supposed to talk about at parties - religion and politics! They are volatile subjects and yet intimately intertwined. I read a blog the other day stating, *"Theological claims are not articulations of personal preference or taste. They are claims about what is objectively true based on a particular understanding of the good. They deserve precisely the same place in public discourse as similar kinds of secular claims."* [Charles C. Camosy, ESSAY: WHAT IT MEANS TO 'GET' RELIGION IN 2020, 16 September

2019] This delves into the world of absolute verses relative values, another hotbed of dispute.

Following God's instruction, Samuel gives the people what they want, but he washes his hands of this decision. *"The Lord is witness against you, and also his anointed is witness this day, that you have not found anything in my hand."* Samuel then reminded them of their checkered history. They have never been consistently obedient, cry out when afflicted, and forget God when things are going well. And to once again demonstrate God's power, Samuel declares that it will rain on their wheat harvest. One commentator states, *"Some people will not be brought to a sight of their sins by any gentler methods than storms and thunders."* [Matthew Henry]

There is a warning in that statement. Israel's history is replete with examples of God's gentle discipline only to be followed by more harsh correction. In pride and arrogance, his people have chosen to pursue their own path. How do we today know the right way? To whom do we listen? In the wake of several mass shootings, political leaders have rightly said that they are praying for the victim's families. This used to be accepted as an appropriate gesture, but like the people seeking a king, today they would rather see political action than invoking spiritual help. St. Augustine said, "Pray as though everything depended on God. Work as though everything depended on you."

Samuel reminded them of God's purpose for them and of his final duty: *"For the sake of his great name the Lord will not reject his people, because the Lord was pleased to make you his own. As for me, far be it from me that I should sin against the Lord by failing to pray for you. And I will teach you the way that is good and right."* Religion grounds a people. It is not an external apparatus thrown on and off based on personal preference. Camosy further says in his blog *"Someone for whom religion is very important doesn't think of it as something like their favorite flavor of ice cream. Their theological claims express things they believe to be objectively true. A particular kind of god exists. That god created the universe. That god made every human being in God's image and likeness. That god commanded men and women to be fruitful and multiply. To give a preference to the poor and marginalized. To welcome the child and the stranger. And so on."* I have chosen Christianity. We all choose something, even if it's a religion of self.

What kind of boss or coworker do you want? One who boasts a purely secular mind, making judgments according to personal biases, or one who is accountable to a holy God? This God has been proven to love us and provide beneficial rules of discipline that are helpful for all people, at all times, in all places.

We will all serve someone. Whose principles do you uphold? Whose values do you support? Upon what basis are they formed?

Application:
1) Do you make decisions with values and principles that are always forming and changing or do you have a solid basis grounded in timeless Truth?
2) Do you recognize the inevitable intersection of religion and politics?
3) Do you remember a time when you received gentle warnings that you did not heed and you only changed because of "storms and thunder"?
4) What does it mean to say to someone, "I'll pray for you" when they are going through a difficult trial?

*   *   *

*"As for me and my household, we will serve the Lord."*
(Joshua 24:15)

# Day 38

We Begin with God's Word

1 Samuel 13:1-15

Saul was thirty years old when he became king, and he reigned over Israel forty-two years. Saul chose three thousand men from Israel; two thousand were with him at Mikmash and in the hill country of Bethel, and a thousand were with Jonathan at Gibeah in Benjamin. The rest of the men he sent back to their homes. Jonathan attacked the Philistine outpost at Geba, and the Philistines heard about it. Then Saul had the trumpet blown throughout the land and said, "Let the Hebrews hear!" So all Israel heard the news: "Saul has attacked the Philistine outpost, and now Israel has become obnoxious to the Philistines." And the people were summoned to join Saul at Gilgal.

The Philistines assembled to fight Israel, with three thousand chariots, six thousand charioteers, and soldiers as numerous as the sand on the seashore. They went up and camped at Mikmash, east of Beth Aven. When the Israelites saw that their situation was critical and that their army was hard pressed, they hid in caves and thickets, among the rocks, and in pits and cisterns. Some Hebrews even crossed the Jordan to the land of Gad and Gilead. Saul remained at Gilgal, and all the troops with him were quaking with fear. He waited seven days, the time set by Samuel; but Samuel did not come to Gilgal, and Saul's men began to scatter. So he said, "Bring me the burnt offering and the fellowship offerings." And Saul offered up the burnt offering. Just as he finished making the offering, Samuel arrived, and Saul went out to greet him.

"What have you done?" asked Samuel. Saul replied, "When I saw that the men were scattering, and that you did not come at the set time, and that the Philistines were assembling at Mikmash, I thought, 'Now the Philistines will come down against me at Gilgal, and I have not sought the Lord's favor.' So I felt compelled to offer the burnt offering." "You have done a foolish thing," Samuel said. "You have not kept the command the Lord your God gave you; if you had, he would have established your kingdom over Israel for all time. But now your kingdom will not endure; the Lord has sought out a man after his own heart and appointed him ruler of his people, because you have not kept the Lord's command." Then Samuel left Gilgal and went up to Gibeah in Benjamin, and Saul counted the men who were with him. They numbered about six hundred.

## Saul: Privileged Position/Poor Attitude

I submitted my resume with a carefully crafted cover letter on Monday and then I waited. I got no response. Did they receive it? When should I follow up? Is a phone call appropriate? What about an email? Do I know anyone within the company that could casually go by the HR office and inquire for me? This is what the job seeker goes through every time they apply for a job. At Career Prospectors, a Richmond-based job-seeking organization, we give all kinds of helpful advice in answer to the above questions. Answers that come from HR professionals and others who have done hiring for a living.

When the position doesn't materialize we may blame ourselves for following up too quickly or not soon enough. Maybe my resume was too long or the wrong format. We might blame others for age discrimination or having a point of view that is short-sighted. We often hear excuses, and sometimes even humility, but it takes awhile to get there since our natural inclination is most often self-defense and pride.

Saul had been king for possibly less than a year before he succumbed to a pride that was nonexistent when he was just a son working for his father. As king, he had thousands at his disposal and, in today's passage he decided to attack the Philistines, a neighboring kingdom who seemed to annoy him. This caused his enemy to react with such vigor that the Israelites all ran and hid in caves and thickets, among the rocks, and in pits and cisterns.

Seeing that their situation was desperate, Saul turned to his Plan B: wait for the prophet Samuel and see what he has to say. Samuel had told him to wait seven days and apparently do nothing, but it seemed that Saul was itching to be king-like, so he attacked the Philistines. On day 7, Samuel had still not arrived, so Saul took matters into his own hands. He'd seen sacrifices done hundreds of times; get the animal, cut its throat, drain the blood, burn its carcass and lift your arms up in the air to God. How hard could it be?

It was not a matter of difficulty but of permission. Only an ordained prophet or priest was allowed to make the sacrifice. This was decreed by God himself. Samuel showed up as he promised and gives Saul a tongue lashing. And what follows is a repeat from the garden of Eden.

Excuses, blame, and justification, is a pattern that we all fall into. We do it to preserve our ego and our image, but it always backfires. *"You did not come at the set time,"* Saul said to Samuel. An excuse and blame all in one, and wrong. *"The people were afraid and scattering."* Saul felt he had to act kingly so as to keep order. And to top it off he tried to impress Samuel with his pious attitude, *"I felt compelled to offer the burnt offering."* In other words, and I hear this so often, "*I felt God calling me to do this*." As if this makes it all better and who can argue with God?

Samuel would have none of it. *"You have done a foolish thing,"* Samuel said. *"You have not kept the command the Lord your God gave you; if you had, he would have established your kingdom over Israel for all time. But now your kingdom will not endure..."* Some might think this judgment was too harsh. As one commentator said, "No, *The Lord is righteous in all his ways* and does no man any wrong, *will be justified when he speaks and clear when he judges*." [Matthew Henry] By this, God shows that there is no such thing as a little sin. James, the half-brother of Jesus says in James 2:10, *"For whoever keeps the whole law and yet stumbles at just one point is guilty of breaking all of it."*

What if Saul had repented? Could this story have had a different ending? But he didn't. We often write our own epitaph, don't we? The beauty of knowing God and his Word, is that there is no mystery as to what he expects of us. The pattern is that, as we acquire knowledge we put it into practice.

What we teach at Career Prospectors are not religious principles but time-honored practices that, if followed, will help one have success. After every Job Expo that we put on, the employers regularly comment that those who are members of our group reflect professionalism and poise. We can help you get a job because following a few rules goes a long way.

As is often the case, a study of Saul teaches us more about what not to do. But flip every prohibition and you will find truth that sets you free. Accept responsibility for your actions, admit when you're wrong and be willing to learn from your mistakes.

Application:
1. How do you handle rejection, from others or a company to which you've applied?
2. What difference does it make whether you accept responsibility for your errors or blame others for their short comings?
3. When have you stepped out of line and done something you weren't supposed to? Did you accept responsibility or make excuses? What was the result?

4. Has someone ever rebuked you like Samuel did to Saul? How did you respond?
5. What have you learned from watching others make mistakes?

\* \* \*

*This is what the Sovereign Lord, the Holy One of Israel, says: "In repentance and rest is your salvation, in quietness and trust is your strength, but you would have none of it."*
(Isaiah 30:15)

# Day 39

We Begin with God's Word

1 Samuel 16:1-13

*The Lord said to Samuel, "How long will you mourn for Saul, since I have rejected him as king over Israel? Fill your horn with oil and be on your way; I am sending you to Jesse of Bethlehem. I have chosen one of his sons to be king." But Samuel said, "How can I go? If Saul hears about it, he will kill me." The Lord said, "Take a heifer with you and say, 'I have come to sacrifice to the Lord.' Invite Jesse to the sacrifice, and I will show you what to do. You are to anoint for me the one I indicate." Samuel did what the Lord said. When he arrived at Bethlehem, the elders of the town trembled when they met him. They asked, "Do you come in peace?"*

*Samuel replied, "Yes, in peace; I have come to sacrifice to the Lord. Consecrate yourselves and come to the sacrifice with me." Then he consecrated Jesse and his sons and invited them to the sacrifice. When they arrived, Samuel saw Eliab and thought, "Surely the Lord's anointed stands here before the Lord." But the Lord said to Samuel, "Do not consider his appearance or his height, for I have rejected him. The Lord does not look at the things people look at. People look at the outward appearance, but the Lord looks at the heart."*

*Then Jesse called Abinadab and had him pass in front of Samuel. But Samuel said, "The Lord has not chosen this one either." Jesse then had Shammah pass by, but Samuel said, "Nor has the Lord chosen this one." Jesse had seven of his sons pass before Samuel, but Samuel said to him, "The Lord has not chosen these." So he asked Jesse, "Are these all the sons you have?" "There is still the youngest," Jesse answered. "He is tending the sheep." Samuel said, "Send for him; we will not sit down until he arrives."*

*So he sent for him and had him brought in. He was glowing with health and had a fine appearance and handsome features. Then the Lord said, "Rise and anoint him; this is the one." So Samuel took the horn of oil and anointed him in the presence of his brothers, and from that day on the Spirit of the Lord came powerfully upon David. Samuel then went to Ramah.*

## Making A New Start

When the wrong person has been hired it seems the company has two options: 1) Fix the problem immediately by letting them go or 2) hope that they will adjust, adapt or otherwise quickly get with the program. In some cases we were that person, in others we had to work with someone who caused us to question our tenure at the company.

King Saul had blown it. He had not revered God as he should by inappropriately offering a sacrifice in Saul's place. "It seemed like a good idea at the time", is what is often said when things don't work out the way we thought they would. Saul had forfeited his role as King of Israel, despite all the effort God and Samuel had put into him. When Samuel anointed Saul with oil the Scriptures said, *'As Saul turned to leave Samuel, God changed Saul's heart, and all these signs were fulfilled that day."* Later on, *"they sacrificed fellowship offerings before the Lord, and Saul and all the Israelites held a great celebration."* This was to celebrate Saul as Israel's first king. Why did things go awry?

Despite being anointed, having his heart changed and having his kingship confirmed by the people through celebration, things just didn't work out for Saul. Many of us have seen this happen in our careers. The "perfect" job doesn't exist. Conflict happens. Expectations were unrealistic. The chemistry wasn't right. How do we move on and not make the same mistake again?

Samuel also had to reevaluate his role as the prophet in Israel. He, as God's prophet and messenger, seemed to have lost his confidence. But God continued to use him, even in his old age. He commanded him to anoint a new king. *"Fill your horn with oil and be on your way; I am sending you to Jesse of Bethlehem. I have chosen one of his sons to be king."* I can imagine Samuel thinking, *"Haven't we been through this before? This didn't go so well last time."* But as one commentator said, *"The people chose the last king...one that looked 'kingly', but God will choose the next one." [Matthew Henry] "The Lord does not look at the things people look at. People look at the outward appearance, but the Lord looks at the heart."*

Samuel and Saul were unique individuals with strengths and weaknesses. Samuel seemed to be qualified for his role, whereas Saul struggled to prove that he really measured up. In our situations, how many times does the interviewer really get to the heart of the matter? How many of us have been hired because of who we are rather than what we can do? My friends in Career Prospectors are good at what they do but they often run into roadblocks: low salary offers, age discrimination, disappointing benefits packages, etc. "If only they would hire me," we think, "I would prove to them that I am worth every penny and my \_\_\_\_\_ is a benefit, not a risk."

Samuel "interviewed" seven of Jesse's sons but God informed him that none of them were THE one. I rarely sympathize with Human Resources, but I can imagine that they face seemingly impossible odds at times. I can imagine that sometimes the right candidate just doesn't seem to exist. They may ask with Samuel, *"Are these all the candidates you have?"* In other words, "Give me a candidate that I can believe in." When David comes in from the fields, God impresses upon Samuel that he is the right person, and not because of his talents or expertise but because of his heart. (Later on the writers of biblical history record David as one who followed God with all his heart). As we get up every day and strive to be a good boss or employee, what is in the forefront of our minds? Trying to do the right thing without a heart and mind set on heavenly things will only produce earthly results.

As with Saul, when Samuel anointed David with oil, the Spirit came mightily upon him. The difference between the two men was that David chose to cooperate with God's Spirit through obedience to his Word. He wasn't perfect but the attitude of his heart enabled him to say, *"keep me as the apple of your eye."*

Application:
1) When we have made mistakes, are we quick to blame someone else, seek a way out or confess in order to make it right?
2) Saul was in a position of privilege and he crashed and burned. How have you handled being chosen above all others?
3) What is the attitude of your heart? Pride and arrogance may be perceived as confidence but it will not take you as far as humility and a servant attitude.
4) What would it look like to view people through the eyes of God in order to make more accurate judgments? We can only do that if we understand him and ourselves as presented in the words of the Bible.

\*    \*    \*

*The Lord does not look at the things people look at. People look at the outward appearance, but the Lord looks at the heart."*
(1 Samuel 16:7)

# Day 40

We Begin with God's Word

Mark 5:1-20

*They went across the lake to the region of the Gerasenes. When Jesus got out of the boat, a man with an impure spirit came from the tombs to meet him. This man lived in the tombs, and no one could bind him anymore, not even with a chain. For he had often been chained hand and foot, but he tore the chains apart and broke the irons on his feet. No one was strong enough to subdue him. Night and day among the tombs and in the hills he would cry out and cut himself with stones. When he saw Jesus from a distance, he ran and fell on his knees in front of him. He shouted at the top of his voice, "What do you want with me, Jesus, Son of the Most High God? In God's name don't torture me!" For Jesus had said to him, "Come out of this man, you impure spirit!"*

*Then Jesus asked him, "What is your name?" "My name is Legion," he replied, "for we are many." And he begged Jesus again and again not to send them out of the area. A large herd of pigs was feeding on the nearby hillside. The demons begged Jesus, "Send us among the pigs; allow us to go into them." He gave them permission, and the impure spirits came out and went into the pigs. The herd, about two thousand in number, rushed down the steep bank into the lake and were drowned.*

*Those tending the pigs ran off and reported this in the town and countryside, and the people went out to see what had happened. When they came to Jesus, they saw the man who had been possessed by the legion of demons, sitting there, dressed and in his right mind; and they were afraid. Those who had seen it told the people what had happened to the demon-possessed man—and told about the pigs as well. Then the people began to plead with Jesus to leave their region.*

*As Jesus was getting into the boat, the man who had been demon-possessed begged to go with him. Jesus did not let him, but said, "Go home to your own people and tell them how much the Lord has done for you, and how he has had mercy on you." So the man went away and began to tell in the Decapolis how much Jesus had done for him. And all the people were amazed.*

## **Rejected by Jesus**
*for a greater purpose*

We try to be confident. We imagine ourselves in positions of authority leading others to profitability and fame. Even if we are unemployed we are coached to proclaim that we are experts in our field and a company would be darn lucky to have us. But what if we are wrong or maybe not 'wrong' but slightly off track? What if there is something better out there waiting for us? And how would we know?

Today's passage is the story of a man who is demon possessed. Jesus asks the demon his name, (this is profound, because he was addressing fallen angels whom Jesus, the Creator, brought into existence eons ago.) The demon was petrified of Jesus because it knew exactly who Jesus was. In verse 7 the man or demon said, *"What do you want with me, Jesus, Son of the Most High God?"* Is this involuntary worship? Do we need any more compelling evidence than a witness from the realms of Heaven and Hell?

The man had been tormented, living among the tombs, cutting himself, being bound hand and foot by the towns people, totally overcome by the forces within him. It makes me wonder how much mental illness is caused by Satan and his minions. I have met people that alternate between different personalities and I calmly proclaim the name of Jesus, the name at which every knee shall bow.

So, Jesus asks its name. *"My name is Legion,"* he replied, *"for we are many."* A legion in the Roman army could have been 500, 5,000 or even 12,000 soldiers. What made this man such a target? It's clear that demonic possession never produced anything good. God created order and beauty. Satan can only distort the good and produce chaos. Nothing original or good. Nothing that this man became was of any use to himself or society. Only terror, distortion of the image of God and fear.

It's in our original makeup to desire to be a contributing member of society. This demon-possessed man had none of that. When we are unemployed we are out of sorts because we are designed to work and to bring order to the world around us. I love hearing the 30-second introductions at the beginning of our Career Prospector meetings. Each one is invariably about creating order from chaos. We are even coached to ask in an interview, "What problems do you have that I can solve for you?"

The demons tried to negotiate with Jesus, playing to his mercy and compassion. *"Send us among the pigs; allow us to go into them."* I'm not sure why that was good, except that it was preferable to being cast into the abyss which comes for all of Satan's army at the end of time. Maybe to their surprise, it still led to destruction.

So often we don't know what's good for us. This is true for these demons but also for the delivered man. *"As Jesus was getting into the boat, the man who had been demon-possessed begged to go with him."* What a natural reaction! You've just met the Messiah, he's delivered you from torment, you want to stay with him. Why not? But Jesus says, "NO." I can't tell you how many times I have imagined the perfect situation, the perfect job, the perfect girlfriend (okay, that goes back a few years), the perfect house, the perfect vacation, the perfect day for golf, etc. And then it seems that God says "No. I have a different plan for you."

We even try to negotiate with God. "God, you don't understand. I need this job. Look at the benefits. I'm perfect for it. God, please, make this work." And then comes the rejection. And maybe not once, but multiple times. God tells the formerly demon possessed man he's got a different job for him to do. *"Go home to your own people and tell them how much the Lord has done for you, and how he has had mercy on you."* Not as glamorous as being with the Messiah but still significant. The man could have disobeyed and chased Jesus all over the country. He could have instead started the "Church of the Tomb" where he had been living all these years. He could have done a number of things and ignored Jesus' command.

He chose to obey. *"So the man went away and began to tell in the Decapolis how much Jesus had done for him. And all the people were amazed."* Each of us was designed to work. We have unique skills and personalities when submitted to the loving hands of our creator will produce the good that God intended. What looks like rejection may mean postponement. It may be protection from a dead-end job or from a toxic work environment. We should be grateful for rejection when things don't work out. It may be the most significant step on the way to discovering the perfect job, spouse, position, etc. that God has for you.

Application:
1. How has rejection produced positive redirection in your life?
2. Describe a time when the best that you could possibly imagine was denied you and yet in hindsight, it was for the best.

3. Have you ever forced a situation after being rejected only to regret it? Would it not have been better to walk away.
4. How do you try to discern God's will for you? Below is a five step outline for seeking God's will:
   1. Pray
   2. Read God's Word
   3. Seek the advice of godly people
   4. Consider the circumstances
   5. Do what you want to do

\* \* \*

*You believe that there is one God. Good! Even the demons believe that—and shudder.*
*(James 2:19)*

## Epilogue

I hope that my musings and observations about God's Word have inspired you to see how practical the Bible is in applying it to everyday life. For some, these past 40 days may have been just the beginning of asking God for purpose in these days of unemployment, waiting and disappointment. If you want additional resources for knowing the God who knows you and the very reason for your existence please contact me at the address below.

Website: www.pickettsweb.info
email: allenpickett@pickettsweb.info

Made in the USA
Columbia, SC
30 March 2020